W0411960

Introduction Welcome to the United States of America 2

Unit 1 New York, New York 6
- Reading Course Part 1 14
- Background File 15
- Working with the text 16
- Checkpoint 1 17

Revision Getting ready for a test 1 18

Unit 2 Both sides of the story 20
- Reading Course Part 2 28
- Background File 29
- Working with the text 30
- Checkpoint 2 31

Selbsteinschätzung 1–2 32

Unit 3 California, land of dreams 34
- Reading Course Part 3 39
- Background File 43
- Working with the text 44
- Checkpoint 3 45

Unit 4 Hermann says 'Willkommen' 46
- Reading Course Part 4 52
- Background File 55
- Working with the text 56
- Checkpoint 4 57

Revision Getting ready for a test 2 58

Selbsteinschätzung 3–4 60

Unit 5 Atlanta rising 62
- Reading Course Part 5 65
- Background File 71
- Working with the text 72
- Checkpoint 5 73

Revision 74

Checkpoint: Lösungen 79

Skills File *kompakt* 84

Grammar File *kompakt* 85

Introduction

Welcome to the United States of America

1 It's fantastic!

▸ pp. 6–7

○* a) *Find words in the box that describe the pictures on pp. 6–7 of your student's book. Write a list.*

amazing • awful • beautiful • boring • colourful • crowded • deep • delicious • exciting • fantastic • foggy • funny • horrible • huge • impressive • natural • noisy • quiet • scary • spicy • terrible • uninteresting • wide • wild

amazing, ______________________________

0201

____

●** b) *Imagine you are at the Grand Canyon and you see the views in the pictures. Use words from your list in a) to write a postcard to a UK friend.*

Dear ...

I'm at the Grand Canyon with my family. It's a huge, deep gorge

____

____

____

____

____

____

____

____

____

Info box

The Skywalk in the west of the Grand Canyon attracts[1] many visitors. The glass floor is 1,220 metres above the canyon floor. That's higher than the world's biggest buildings.

[1] attract [ə'trækt] *locken, anziehen*

*○ leichte Übung **● schwierige Übung

2 New faces ▸ p. 13

a) Fill in their profiles[1].

Name: *Caitlin* ______ ______ ______ ______

Hometown: ______ ______ ______ ______ ______

State: ______ ______ ______ ______ ______

Test

b) Answer these questions about the five students Tick (✓) the correct box.

		Caitlin	Gracie	Luis	Jake	Madison
1	Who made the trip to the Grand Canyon by car with his/her father?				✓	
2	Who flew to Las Vegas first?					
3	Who went to the Grand Canyon with a youth group?					
4	Who travelled almost 2,500 miles by car?					
5	Who took Route 66 to the Grand Canyon?					
6	Who did a six-hour hike to a reservation and rode back?					
7	Who rode with a mule train to the bottom of the Canyon?					
8	Who did lots of jobs to get enough money for the trip?					
9	Who camped at two different places on the rim?					
10	Who went on a two-day hike into the Canyon with his/her dad?					
11	Who visited an old Native American ruin?					

3 WORDS The Grand Canyon puzzle ▸ p. 13

Complete with words from pp. 9–13 of your student's book.

1 The English word for 'eindrucksvoll, beeindruckend' is ...

2 You can walk along the ... of the Canyon or take a bus.

3 If you ... into the Canyon, wear strong shoes and take lots of water.

4 The English word for 'Schlucht' is ...

5 Luis and his friends slept in a ... and cooked their own food.

0303 *6* The Kaibab is a difficult ... into the Canyon.

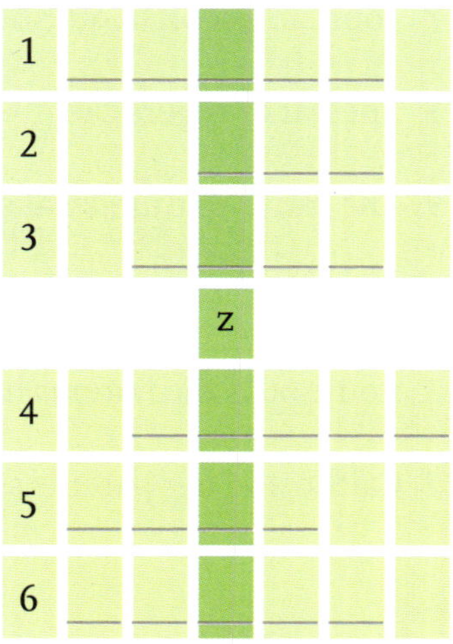

[1] profile ['prəʊfaɪl]

4 The Grand Canyon – right or wrong? ▸ p. 13

Test

a) Are the following statements right or wrong? Mark a number.

	Right	Wrong
1 When you drive from New York to the Grand Canyon you cross four time zones.	70	75
2 Some Native Americans still live in the Grand Canyon.	25	20
3 You are not allowed to camp in the Grand Canyon area.	54	35
4 The Grand Canyon is in the state of Nevada.	30	65
5 The river that goes through the Canyon is the Colorado River.	58	90
6 Las Vegas is in the same state as the Grand Canyon.	15	22
7 You can travel on Route 66 from Chicago to the Canyon.	36	43
8 You can take a mule train into the Canyon.	65	57
9 The park rangers give visitors lots of information about their work.	30	25
10 About 3 million tourists visit the Grand Canyon every year.	65	35

b) Add the ten numbers that are marked and write the answer: ________ . The correct answer tells you how long the Grand Canyon is in kilometres. Check your answer on p. 8 of your student's book.

5 STUDY SKILLS Correcting mistakes ▸ p. 13 • SF (p. 169)

Find and mark the grammar and spelling mistakes. There's one in each sentence. Then write what is correct.

	Correct
1 Luis worked hardly to get enough money for his trip to the Grand Canyon.	hard
2 Jake and his dad have begun their journey on August 7th.	
3 Acommodation at the Canyon is no problem. There are hotels, motels, campsites.	
4 In the bus Luis and his friends sang songs and talked to themselves all the time.	
5 The Kruger's trip on Route 66 took them through five states.	
6 When they arrived at the Canyon, Jake and his dad were on the road for four days.	
7 Tourists ask often questions about the history of the Canyon.	
8 The park rangers can give you lots of informations about the Canyon.	
9 The multi-coloured walls of the Canyon look beautifully in the sun.	
10 Jake's dad is a good driver. He drives really good.	
11 Route 66 is the famous highway who goes from Chicago to L.A.	
12 Caitlin and her parents always go in summer to a national park.	

0405

6 STUDY SKILLS WRITING A Grand Canyon blog ▸ p. 13 • SF (pp. 168–169)

Imagine that you went to the Grand Canyon in your summer vacation. Use the information that the five students in your student's book give about the Canyon and the pictures. Write your own short blog. For ideas look at Caitlin's blog on p. 9 of your student's book. Write about 100–120 words in your exercise book.

Remember your writing skills:

- *brainstorm your ideas (mind map, list)*
- *structure your text (beginning, middle, end)*
- *use paragraphs (a new paragraph for a new idea)*
- *structure your information (5 Ws: Who? What? When? Where? Why? + How?)*
- *make your sentences interesting (use linking words, adjectives, adverbs, relative clauses)*
- *read your text and correct your mistakes (grammar, spelling)*

7 The Grand Canyon quiz ▸ p. 13

a) *What have you learned about the Grand Canyon? Tick (✔) the correct answer, A, B or C. You need the letters in brackets in part b).*

1 In which US state is the Grand Canyon?

A Nevada. (D)	B California. (C)	✔ Arizona. (O)

2 What time is it in the Canyon when it's 11 o'clock in Atlanta?

A 8 o'clock. (R)	B 9 o'clock. (O)	C 10 o'clock. (P)

3 About how deep is the Grand Canyon?

A A kilometre. (N)	B A mile. (A)	C More than a mile. (R)

4 About how long is the Grand Canyon?

A 277 kilometres. (O)	B 277 miles. (D)	C 25 kilometres. (A)

5 In which year was the Grand Canyon made a national park?

A 1919. (N)	B 1909. (B)	C 1929. (C)

6 What is the Wampanoag?

A A river. (E)	B A Native American tribe. (C)	C A Native American ruin. (S)

b) *Now write the letters in brackets next to your answers in the boxes below. If your answers are correct, the letters make the name of something Jake saw in the Canyon. Here are the question numbers:*

6	1	5	4	2	3
	O				

Extra Now you

Use the internet to prepare a two-minute talk[1] on the state of Arizona. How big is it? How many people live there? What's the weather like? What tourist attractions[2] can you find there? What do you know about the Native Americans who live there? Make notes in your exercise book and practise your talk.

0509

[1] talk *Rede, Vortrag* [2] attraction [ə'trækʃn]

Unit 1 New York, New York

1 About New York ► pp. 14–15

Test

On the bike tour Ryan learns a lot of facts about New York. Are the statements right or wrong? Mark a letter.

		Right	Wrong
1	New York is called the Big Apple.	I	S
2	New York has lots of cycle paths, so it's a safe city for bikers.	A	I
3	Protests[1] in New York often take place at Washington Square.	A	F
4	You are not allowed to cycle across Washington Square.	E	T
5	Many Irish people left their country and came to New York in the 1890s.	E	U
6	The Statue of Liberty stands on Ellis Island.	M	T
7	All immigrants, rich and poor, had to go through Ellis Island.	L	E
8	The ferry to Staten Island goes right past the Statue of Liberty.	N	T
9	In the 1600s New York belonged to the French.	T	H
10	Chinatown is in Manhattan.	V	S
11	The Brooklyn Bridge goes over the East River.	F	N

Put the letters that are marked in the correct order to make the name of a famous street in New York that Ryan did not visit on the bike tour:

____

2 Blue box: New York's boroughs ► p. 15, p. 22/P1, p. 198

Test

What do you know about New York's boroughs? Tick (✔) the correct letter, A, B or C.

1 Look at the picture. Which borough does it show?

A Queens. B Manhattan. C Brooklyn.

2 The Bronx is … of Manhattan. A south B east C north

3 The biggest New York borough is … A Queens. B Brooklyn. C Staten Island.

4 Which two boroughs are on Long Island?

A The Bronx and Manhattan. B The Bronx and Queens. C Queens and Brooklyn.

5 In which borough is Kennedy Airport? A Manhattan. B Queens. C Brooklyn.

6 There's a free ferry between …

A Brooklyn and Ellis Island. B Manhattan and Liberty Island. C Staten Island and Manhattan.

[1] protest ['prəʊtest]

3 LISTENING All about ... getting around an American city ▸ p. 16 • SF (p. 161) Track 2

Test

You are in Manhattan and you want to go to the Brooklyn Bridge. Look at the map and listen. Which person gives you the right directions? A, B or C?

Fun fact

Brooklyn Bridge is the only bridge where... a plane could fly over a pedestrian who was walking over a car that was driving over a boat that was sailing[1] over a train. (The subway runs under the East River.)

The person who gives the right directions is ______ .

4 WORDS Tourists in New York ▸ p. 16

a) *Read the lists carefully. What goes together? Draw lines to match.*

1	ask	time • money
2	spend	the way • questions
3	see	information • help
4	look round	the sights • a film
5	ask for	museums • shops

b) *Choose the correct word(s) from a) to complete the sentences.*

1 On clear days tourists always ____________ time on top of the ESB.

2 They usually want to ____________ Macy's[2].

3 Lots of visitors get lost and have to ____________ the way.

4 Many tourists ____________ at the subway ticket machines.

5 Some tourists try to ____________ in just one day.

[1] sail [seɪl] *segeln* [2] Macy's ['meɪsi:z] *großes Kaufhaus in New York*

5 Blue box: American English (I) ▸ p. 16, p. 194

a) Which words are British English (BE)? Which words are American English (AE)? Find and write pairs.

mobile phone	sidewalk	gas	flat	lift	subway
elevator	take a left	downtown	holiday(s)	gas station	dollar
line	city centre	underground	pound	queue	cellphone
vacation	petrol station	class	petrol	grade	pavement
		turn left	apartment		

mobile phone – cellphone

0805

b) Ryan wrote these sentences in an e-mail to a friend back home. Underline the word in each sentence that is different in American English spelling. How would Caitlin write the words?

AE

1 I travelled to New York by plane, of course. — traveled

2 Travelling is hard work!

3 I'd like to go to a theatre on Broadway.

4 I'd like to see *The Phantom of the Opera*. It's my favourite musical.

5 The ice cream here is great. They've got lots of cool flavours.

6 The Statue of Liberty is 93 metres high!

7 Next week we're going to do a harbour trip.

8 Broadway is the longest street in New York City – it's 29 kilometres long!

6 WORDS Talking about jobs ▸ p. 17

a) Write the job names under the pictures.

actor • *artist* • caretaker • coach • editor • firefighter • journalist • TV presenter

artist ________ ________ ________

0906

________ ________ ________ ________

b) Which of the people in the photos has the most interesting job? Who probably has the most boring job? In your exercise book, write what you think and why in 80–100 words.

I think the ... probably has the most interesting job because ...

I think the ... has the most boring job because ...

Info box

New York City is often called 'The city that never sleeps'. With a population of over 8 million it's the biggest city in the USA – the second largest city is Los Angeles. On the streets of New York about 170 languages are spoken.

7 Sightseeing (Gerund as subject) ▸ p. 17 • GF 1 a–b (p. 173)

Write the gerunds of these verbs. Then choose the correct gerund to complete what Ryan and Caitlin say.

plan – *planning* shop – ________

get – ________ visit – ________

cycle – ________ walk – ________

run – ________ write – ________

Ryan *Planning* things to do in New York is fun. I'm really excited. How are we going to get around?

Caitlin Well, ________ is fun. But ________ around the city is quicker by bus or subway. We can't cycle all the time, and ________ soon makes you tired. ________ in Central Park is fun too. We could do that if you like.

Ryan Sure, but ________ all the famous sights is more important first.

And ________ at Macy's is important too. I need some presents for my family and I have to write postcards to all my friends.

0907 *Caitlin* ________ postcards is boring. But I'm sure we'll have enough time for Macy's!

8 He loves being a firefighter (Gerund as object)

▸ p. 17 • GF 1 a–b (p. 173)

Use a gerund to make one sentence out of two.

1 Caitlin's dad is a New York firefighter. He loves his job.

Caitlin's dad loves being a New York firefighter.

2 He sometimes gets up in the middle of the night. He doesn't like that.

____

3 Ryan thinks New York is great, but he couldn't live there. He can't imagine it.

____

4 Caitlin often rides her bike in the rain. She enjoys it.

____

5 Caitlin's mom often shops at Macy's. She really likes that.

____

6 Visitors to New York always go up the Empire State Building. They love it.

____

7 But Ryan doesn't usually go in fast lifts. He hates it.

1008 ______________________________

9 LISTENING Blue box: American English (II)

▸ p. 18, p. 198 Track 3

a) Different words

Listen to the American English (AE) words and write them down. Then write the British English (BE) words next to them.

AE		BE
1 eraser	–	
2	–	
3	–	
4	–	
5	–	
6	–	

b) Different pronunciation

Listen to the words. Is the pronunciation BE or AE? Write **BE** *or* **AE** *after the number.*

1 AE	6
2	7
3	8
4	9
5	10

10 Liam (Gerund after prepositions) ▸ p. 18 • GF 1 c (p. 174)

Ryan's cousin Liam in Ireland talks about New York Choose a gerund of the verbs in the list to complete the sentences.

be • get • *go* • join • live • make • meet • move • not speak • work

'I was lucky. I had the chance of *going* to New York on a student exchange. I'm even interested in ______ a job there. I've often dreamt of ______ to another country. I really like the idea of ______ in a big city office[1] in New York – and I needn't worry about ______ the language. At first I might be a bit scared of ______ alone without friends, but I could always visit my exchange family. I'm quite good at ______ friends and I'd have the chance of ______ lots of new people at work. I'd soon find out about ______
1110 a sports club or a youth group. I'd never be tired of ______ in the city that never sleeps.'

11 Blue box: Verbs with two objects ▸ p. 18, p. 195

Complete the sentences with **to** *where necessary.*

1 Caitlin showed ______ Ryan lots of interesting places in the city.
2 She explained ______ him how to buy subway tickets.
3 Caitlin's mom gave ______ Ryan a pocket map of the city.
4 Caitlin's dad described the work of NY firefighters ______ him.
5 Ryan sent ______ his friends lots of postcards.
6 He's going to do a project on New York and present it ______ the class.

12 EVERYDAY ENGLISH SPEAKING Visiting Liberty ▸ p. 19 Track 4

It's your first day in New York. Your exchange partner Todd asks you what you would like to do. You'd like to see the Statue of Liberty first. Listen to Todd and give suitable[2] answers or comments in the pauses. Say as much as you can. Use the ideas below or your own ideas. Do the exercise at least twice. First read the Fun fact box.

1 you want to see everything – start with Liberty
2 yes, of course – from parents – last birthday
3 read a lot – know some details (see Fun fact!)
4 yes – school history lessons – immigration station – reasons for immigration

Fun fact

The Statue of Liberty

- was born on 28th October 1886
- is 93 m tall
- weighs 204,100 kilos
- her nose is almost 1.5 m long
- her feet are 7.6 m long, so she takes size 879 sandals[3]
- you can climb 354 stairs (22 floors) to the crown[4], but since 9/11 it has been closed to visitors

[1] office ['ɒfɪs] *Büro* [2] suitable ['sju:təbl] *passend, geeignet* [3] sandal ['sændl] *Sandale* [4] crown [kraʊn] *Krone*

13 WORDS New York puzzle ▸ p. 19

Write the answers in the puzzle and find a famous name for New York.

1 This borough has a famous zoo. It's the …

2 New Yorkers often buy food and coffee to go here.

3 The name for the place where the towers of the World Trade Center stood is '… Zero'.

4 New Yorkers often have this for breakfast.

5 The World Trade Center burned and … on 9/11/2001.

6 The 'E' in ESB means …

7 A famous bridge links this borough to Manhattan.

1213 8 The bridge in 7 goes over the … River.

Now you

What do you know about 'Ground Zero'? Prepare a three-minute talk for class. Use the information on p. 17 of your student's book and look for more information on the internet. Make notes, then practise your talk.

14 WRITING My trip to the ESB ▸ p. 19 • SF (pp. 168–169)

Test

Imagine you went up the Empire State Building. In your exercise book, write a short report about your visit (about 150 words). Read p. 18 of your student's book again first.

Remember the steps of writing:

1 Brainstorming ideas
- collect ideas and put them in order (in a list, mind map)
- answer the questions Who? What? When? Where? Why? and maybe How? (in a chart)

2 Writing
- structure your text (beginning, middle, end)
- use paragraphs and topic sentences
- write better sentences with adjectives, adverbs, time phrases, linking words, relative clauses

3 Revising and correcting your text
- think carefully about spelling (e.g. take > taking, plan > planned, half > halves)
- be careful with grammar (tenses, verb endings, irregular verbs, word order)

These phrases will help you:

summer holidays • visit e-friend • weather great, so … • wait in long queue • fast lift to top • good visibility • fantastic views • ESB facts • take photos • write postcards • buy souvenirs • exciting visit

15 EVERYDAY ENGLISH Times Square (Mediating spoken information) ▸ p. 19 • SF (p. 165)

Test

You are in New York. A young German tourist asks you the way to Times Square, but you don't know, so you ask an American woman on the street. Mediate, but remember you don't have to translate every word.

You Times Square? Ich weiß es leider auch nicht. Aber ich frage jemanden. Moment.

Excuse me, this guy is a tourist and he wants to know the way to Times Square.

I'm a tourist too, so I'm afraid I can't tell him.

Woman Oh, OK. Now let's see. Times Square isn't far from here. But it's getting dark, so it would be better to take the subway or a bus. There's a subway station just round the corner.

You Sie sagt, Times Square ist nicht weit, ______________________

____

Tourist Nein, nein, ich möchte zu Fuß gehen. Ich habe ein bisschen Angst, mit der U-Bahn zu fahren. Mein Englisch ist nicht gut, und ich kenne mich mit den Bussen auch nicht aus.

You He says ______________________

____

Woman OK. Well, we're on 48th Street right now, close to the Rockefeller Center, so he needs to get onto Sixth Avenue and go south. It's that way. When he's on Sixth Avenue – which is also called Avenue of the Americas – he should go straight on about four or five blocks, then take a right into 43rd. Then straight down 43rd and he'll see Times Square on the left. You can't miss the bright lights. Is that OK?

You OK. Sie meint, wir sind in der Nähe vom Rockefeller Center, und du gehst in diese

Richtung zur ______________________

____

____

____

Tourist OK. Frag sie bitte, wie weit es ist und wie lange ich brauchen werde.

You He wants to know how ______________________

Woman Oh, it's about half a mile. It will take about ten minutes. Sorry, I have to hurry now, but good luck!

You ______________________

____

____

Tourist OK. Danke. Thank you!

1315 *You* Wiedersehen und viel Spaß!

Info box

Times Square

Times Square got its name from the *New York Times* newspaper building, which stood there in 1904.
Today you find bright lights, cinemas, theatres, shops, bars and restaurants there.
On New Year's Eve[1] thousands of people meet in Times Square to celebrate[2].

[1] New Year's Eve ['iːv] *Silvester* [2] celebrate ['selɪbreɪt] *feiern*

16 READING COURSE
Part 1: Visit downtown New York (Working out the meaning of words) ▸ p. 19 • SF (p. 163)

a) Read this part of a tourist brochure. Think about the underlined words.

Visit downtown New York

Some things have changed, but a lot have remained the same in downtown New York. It's an important center of commerce and has more than 300 years of history.

Downtown has lots of art galleries and museums, architecture, skyscrapers, concert halls, technology, shopping malls, lots of restaurants, entertainment and great waterfront.

Don't miss the sunset over the Hudson – it's a must.

There are so many sights to see. The excitement and energy of the city is endless.

You can get there by bus, car or subway. It takes only 20 minutes to walk from the Hudson to the East River. Why not take a luxury ride in a stretch limo?

The food downtown is varied, as New Yorkers will tell you. It is served leisurely or fast. You can eat indoors or out. Or why not dine in elegance?

Get a hot dog from a street vendor or bagels from a deli.

And you'll never be bored. There's always lots of fun. Just enjoy the sounds and smells of downtown New York.

b) Which techniques helped you to understand the new words? Write the words in four lists:

1 The pictures help me to understand these words:

vendor (Verkäufer), ______

______

2 These words look like German (or French or Latin) words:

commerce (Handel, Kommerz), ______

______

______

3 I can understand these words from the context:

changed (sich verändern) ______

4 I already know a part of the word or a word from the word family:

______

______

17 Extra Background File ALL STRANGERS ▸ pp. 20–21

a) Read the statements of the five immigrant children on p. 20 of your student's book, then read 1–5 below. Who said what? Write the name.

1 This child felt very small when he/she first saw the big building on Ellis Island. The child's name was ______________________.

2 This immigrant said that at first they had lived near the East River in a dark building with lots of other people. This person's name was ______________________.

3 This child said that everything had been strange to them when they arrived in the US. People had known nothing about the new country they had come to. The child was ______________________.

4 This immigrant said that they were all strangers, so nobody really felt like a stranger. This child was ______________________.

5 This immigrant said the weather at sea had been terrible, so they were very happy when they came into the bay of New York. This child's name was ______________________.

Test

b) What do you know about Ellis Island and US immigrants? Tick (✔) the correct answer, A, B or C. Sometimes more than one answer is correct. You need the letters in brackets in c).

1 When was the Ellis Island Immigration Station opened? A 1892. (S) B 1900. (I) C 1921. (H)

2 Why did some immigrants leave their homes to go to America?
A They were poor and hungry at home. (I)
B For reasons of religion or politics. (S)
C The US paid immigrant workers well. (G)

3 How many immigrants came to the US between 1892 and 1924?
A 4 million. (L) B More than 12 million. (A) C 76 million. (R)

4 What is Ellis Island today? A An immigration station. (I) B A castle. (S) C A museum. (U)

5 In the year 2000, how many per cent of the US population were immigrants?
A 13.6%. (I) B 9.18%. (S) C 10.8%. (R)

c) The letters after the correct answers in b) tell you the name of a country where many immigrants came from. Put the letters in the correct order.

The country is ______________.

d) Use the information on pp. 20–21 of your student's book and write a report (about 150 words) with the title 'Immigration to the US from 1892 to the present'. You can use the website www.ellisisland.org to find out more information.

18 WORKING WITH THE TEXT The writer and the firefighter ▸ pp. 28–30

a) Understanding what happens. Answer these questions in one or two sentences each.

1 What does Nick have to do? ______

2 Why is this job so difficult for him? ______

3 What does he tell Joan about Bill? ______

4 How does Joan help Nick? ______

b) Understanding what they say. Find the following lines in the text on pp. 28–30. What do you think the speakers really mean? Tick (✔) A or B.

1 Why does Joan's father ask the question in ll. 11–12?

A Joan's father can't believe that anyone would do such a terrible thing.

B Joan's father also believes that it was terrorism and wants to know the reasons for it.

2 Why does Nick say he is no writer in ll. 51–52?

A Nick says he's a firefighter, not a writer. B Nick says he isn't good at writing.

3 In ll. 78–80, why does Nick give this opinion about the media?

A Nick thinks it's good that the media talk and write about the dead firefighters as heroes all the time.

B Nick doesn't like the way the media report on the dead firefighters because they say nothing personal about them.

4 What does Nick say about Bill in ll. 116–117?

A Bill always helped the new firefighters with their work. B Bill liked to be the boss.

c) Using new words. Use these words and phrases from the play to make true sentences.

1 terrorism: *When Joan heard the news about the World Trade Center, she thought it was maybe terrorism.*

2 comfort: ______

3 dependable: ______

4 noble: ______

d) **Extra** *If a journalist interviewed Nick about what happened to him and his men on 9/11, what do you think he would ask? Write six questions. (Remember: Who? What? Where? When? Why? How? and Yes/No questions). Write in your exercise book.*

1 American English. What are these places?

1 You can buy sandwiches, snacks and coffee to go here. ______

2 This is what Americans call the city centre. ______

3 You can see lots of these very tall buildings in American cities. ______

4 This is what Americans call the distance from one street to the next. ______

1701 5 In the US you buy petrol here. ______

2 British and American English. Write the missing words.

BE	AE	BE	AE
1 holiday(s) –	______	4 pavement –	______
2 queue –	______	5 ground floor –	______
3 timetable –	______	6 (school) year –	______

1702

3 Complete the sentences with gerunds of the verbs in the box.

find • meet • plan • take • travel

1 Caitlin really enjoyed ______ a sightseeing tour of New York for Ryan.

2 She had the idea of ______ Ruth and going to Ruth's favourite deli for bagels.

3 Ryan was very interested in ______ out about his uncle's life as a New York firefighter.

4 Ryan enjoyed ______ photos from the top of the Empire State Building.

1703 5 When Ryan was back[1] in Ireland, he often talked about ______ to New York again.

4 STUDY SKILLS Working out the meaning of words

What do the underlined words mean? Use your reading techniques and translate the words into German.

More than a hundred million Americans have ancestors[(1)] who came through Ellis Island. The reasons for the greatest migration in modern history were religious persecution[(2)], political troubles, unemployment[(3)] and adventure. From 1892 to 1924 shipload[(4)] after shipload, mostly Europeans, took their first steps towards becoming Americans.

1704 1 ______ 2 ______ 3 ______ 4 ______

20 points

Now you

1705 1706 *Prepare a short talk about the good things and bad things about life in New York. Make notes or a mind map in your exercise book first. You can use the information in Unit 1 of your student's book and/or information from the internet.*

[1] back [bæk] *zurück*

Here are some exercises that will help you with your practice test 1.

1 WORDS City travel ▸ pp. 32–33

a) *In your exercise book make a 'city travel' network. Look at the pictures for ideas. Use nouns, adjectives and verbs in your network.*

A

B

C

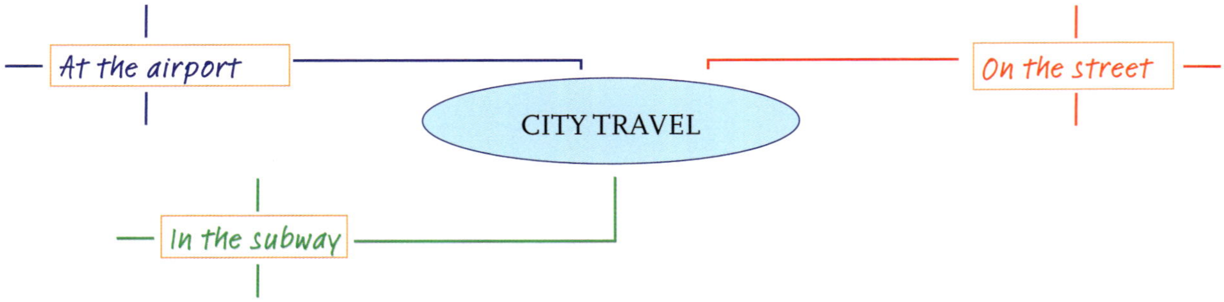

b) *Choose picture A, B or C and describe it in a paragraph. Use* **in the foreground/background, on the right,** *etc.*

Picture ___ shows a scene ____

____

____

____

____

____

____

2 The city that never sleeps (Simple present or present progressive) ▸ pp. 32–33 • Revision 3 (p. 74)

Complete with the correct verb form: simple present or present progressive.

1 The first thing that tourists visit (visit) in New York is the Statue of Liberty or the ESB.

2 Most tourists ______________ (not have) enough time for the museums or the parks.

3 I often ________ (eat) at a deli. I usually __________ (have) a bagel with cream cheese. Delicious!

4 I __________ (go) to my favourite deli right now. My friends ______________ (wait) for me there.

5 It ______________ (rain) now, but later we ______________ (go) to Central Park to hang out.

6 Life in New York ____________ (not get) boring because it's the city that never ________ (sleep).

3 A trip to Macy's (Simple past or past progressive) ▸ pp. 32–33 • Revision 5 (p. 75)

Underline the correct verb form.

Anna, a British exchange student, (stayed/was staying) in New York. Kelly, Anna's exchange partner, (wanted/was wanting) to show her Macy's. Just as they (were crossing/crossed) W 34th Street, Kelly (was saying/said), 'I have to go somewhere for my mom first. I'll meet you in Macy's on the first floor near the elevators in fifteen minutes. OK?'

First, Anna (looked/was looking) at some trendy bags and some funny postcards. Then she (went/was going) to the meeting place. She (was waiting/waited) – 10 minutes, 15 minutes, 20 minutes. But Kelly (didn't arrive/wasn't arriving). What was wrong? Anna (was deciding/decided) to look for Kelly outside. Just as Anna (was walking/walked) downstairs to the main door, she suddenly (saw/was seeing) Kelly. She (stood/was standing) near the elevators. 'But Kelly! You said the first floor! That's one floor up.' 'No, Anna. This is the first floor. You were on the second floor!'

4 STUDY SKILLS Correcting mistakes ▸ pp. 32–33 • SF (p. 169)

This is Jürgen's e-mail to a friend in the States. Mark and correct his mistakes.

	Correct
Hi Todd!	
I am in Berlin since a week. We visit my grandparents here. On	have been, for,
Monday we have seen the Reichstag. It was great. Maybe tomorrow we	
go to the zoo because I enjoy to watch wild animals. We also saw the	
Brandenburg Gate and I made a lot of photos.	
My dad is born in Berlin. When he was a child, lived he in the east part	
of the city. He has told us a lot over the history from the city.	
Just now we sit in a café on the Ku'damm. Dad is takeing photos and	
my sister is shoping. You should visit Berlin too. You'd like it here ...	

5 When I'm in a big city, ... (Gerunds) ▸ pp. 32–33 • GF 1 (pp. 173–174)

Complete the sentences. Use a gerund and your own ideas.

When I'm in a big city for the first time, ...

1 I always enjoy *exploring new places.*

2 I'm always interested in ______

3 I'm sometimes a bit scared of ______

4 I love ______

5 I hate ______

6 I'm always excited about ______

Unit 2 Both sides of the story

1 Patuxet and Plymouth ▸ pp. 36–37

Test

a) Read pp. 36–37 in your student's book again. Have you listened to 'A day in the life of …' in your student's book on p. 36? If yes, then mark a letter.

		Right	Wrong
1	The villages of Patuxet and Plymouth were not in the same place.	S	C
2	The Wampanoag village was called Plymouth.	T	S
3	The English colony was called Plymouth.	H	B
4	Sarah Morton's family had left England because they wanted religious freedom[1].	A	E
5	In 1615 about 1000 Wampanoag Indians lived in Patuxet.	F	M
6	The Wampanoag had corn, squash and beans in their fields.	T	U
7	Sarah Morton has a strict daily routine.	U	R
8	Sarah doesn't have time to learn to read and write.	D	A
9	Tapenum's main daily activity is hunting.	S	N
10	Tapenum comes home with a turkey.	R	T
11	Sarah milks the goats once a day in the morning.	O	E
12	Maybe a terrible illness killed many people in the Wampanoag villages.	S	P
13	When the colonists arrived, the village of Patuxet had already disappeared.	S	Y

b) Put the letters that are marked in the correct order. If your answers are correct, they give you the name of a US state:

____

c) Use a relative clause to paraphrase the words. Make short and clear descriptions to read out in class.

1 turkey: *It's a large bird that people cook for dinner, traditionally at Thanksgiving in the USA.*

2 bow and arrow: ____________________

3 goat: ____________________

4 tablecloth: ____________________

5 spring: ____________________

d) Whose life do you think was more interesting, Tapenum's or Sarah's? Why? In your exercise book, give reasons and write your ideas in a paragraph.

I think … life was more interesting because …

[1] freedom ['fri:dəm] *Freiheit*

2 All about ... history An American timeline ▸ p. 38

Find out when the following important events in American history took place. Use your student's book, the internet and your dictionary and write one or two sentences in the right box. Use the simple present.

US immigration • moon landing • Mayflower • American Revolution[1] • Gold Rush • ~~Columbus~~

Christopher Columbus lands in the New World.

1492 – 1620 – 1776–1783 – 1848 – 1892–1924 – 1969

3 WORDS Causes and effects: The Mayflower ▸ p. 38

Complete with a word/phrase from the box.

the reason why • so (2x) • led to • because of • ~~as a result~~ • as a consequence

Under King James I of England, a religious group called the Puritans[2] were not allowed to practise their religion as they wanted. They wanted to change some things in the Church of England. But critics of the king and the church were very unpopular, and as a result some people lost their lives. This ______ much fear in the Puritan population, ______ a small group decided to join the English settlers in Virginia to have a free and better life. In August 1620 the group left England in two ships, the Mayflower and the Speedwell. But they found out that the Speedwell was not strong enough for the long journey, ______ they had to go back. That's ______ the Mayflower sailed alone from Plymouth on September 6th, with 101 passengers and 30 crew. The maps they had were not good and the weather at sea was often stormy. ______ they landed almost 600 miles north of Virginia, at Cape Cod in Massachusetts. They arrived on November 21st. The Mayflower had taken 66 days to cross the Atlantic ______ the bad weather and many other problems that they had had on the journey.

[1] revolution [ˌrevəˈluːʃn] [2] Puritan [ˈpjʊərɪtən] *Puritaner/in*

4 REVISION Gracie's presentation (Conditional sentences 1)

▸ p. 39 • GF 2a (p. 175)

What do Gracie and her dad say? Complete their sentences with verbs from the box in the correct form.

If we *go* to Plimoth Plantation, you *'ll get/'ll find out* the true facts about the First Thanksgiving. If you ______ questions, the people who work there ______ you correct answers.

get • *go*
give • do
be able to
find out • ask
be • have

Yes, I ______ to prepare my presentation if I ______ enough details. And Mrs Tripp ______ happy if I ______ a good presentation.

2204

5 REVISION Mike would go if he could ... (Conditional sentences 2)

▸ p. 39 • GF 2b (p. 175)

a) *Complete the sentences with the correct forms of the verbs.*

1 If he could, Mike *would go* (go) to Plimoth for the big Thanksgiving Parade.

2 If you ever ______ (go) to Massachusetts, ______ (you, visit) Plimoth Plantation?

3 ______ (you, go) to the Thanksgiving Parade if someone ______ (invite) you?

4 I ______ (ask) Gracie lots of questions about the Wampanoag if she ______ (be) in my class.

2205 5 If I ______ (go) to school in the US, I ______ (be) interested in learning about the American Revolution too.

b) **Extra** *If you had to do a presentation on an American history topic, what would you choose and why? Look at the topics in exercise 2 (p. 21) for ideas. How would you prepare your topic? Write a paragraph in your exercise book.*

6 REVISION Gracie's bad day (Past perfect)

▸ p. 39

a) *Match the sentence halves.*

1 When Gracie got up, she was tired	because she had interrupted his lesson.
2 When she had got ready for school	she left home in a hurry.
3 On the way to school she realized that	the first lesson had already started.
4 When she finally arrived at school,	because she had gone to bed too late.
5 Gracie's Maths teacher wasn't very happy	she had forgotten her money.

b) *Now finish the sentences. Use a verb in the past perfect.*

1 Gracie was hungry in the first lesson because *she hadn't had time for breakfast.*

2 In Mrs Tripp's lesson Gracie got angry with Mike after ______

3 Mrs Tripp got angry with Gracie because ______

4 Gracie and Mike were not very happy because ______

Just for fun

Boy My English teacher punished[1] me for something I hadn't done.
Dad Really? What was it that you hadn't done?
Boy My English essay.

7 What would they have done if ...? (Conditional sentences 3) ▸ p. 39 • GF 2c (p. 176)

Complete the sentences with correct verb forms for conditional sentences (type 3).

1 We weren't free to practise our religion, so we left England. *If we had been free, we wouldn't have left our country.*

2 The Speedwell wasn't strong enough, so the Mayflower sailed alone.

If the Speedwell had been strong enough, the Mayflower ______________________

3 The weather was stormy, so the Mayflower took 66 days to cross the Atlantic.

If the weather ______________________, the Mayflower ______________________ 66 days to cross the Atlantic.

4 We didn't land in Virginia because we didn't have good maps.

We ______________________

5 We built our village here because the water and the land were good.

____

6 We survived the winter because the Wampanoag helped us.

2207

____

Now you

What would you have done? Read p. 39 in your student's book again. What would you/wouldn't you have done or said if you had been Gracie, Mike, Mrs Tripp, Gracie's mom or Gracie's dad? Choose three people and write two sentences for each person in your exercise book.

Gracie: *If I had been Gracie, I wouldn't have got so angry with Mike. I would have been quiet in class, and maybe I would have been rude to Mike in the break. / ... I would have done the same as Gracie.*

8 PRONUNCIATION The same or different? ▸ p. 39 Track 5

Do the underlined parts sound the same? Write Yes or No. Then listen to check your answers.

1 instead	–	bean	*No*	5 maize	–	against	
2 lead	–	spread		6 birth	–	worse	
3 beef	–	bean		7 sweat	–	cream	
4 Jewish	–	queue		8 instead	–	death	

2308

[1] punish ['pʌnɪʃ] bestrafen

9 WORDS Word building

▸ p. 39

Complete the lists. Then use words from the lists in the correct form to complete the sentences below.

NOUN	VERB
survival	survive
cause	______
______	celebrate
______	taste
______	pray

NOUN	ADJECTIVE
danger	______
religion	______
______	surprised
______	dead
______	secret

1 Have you ever eaten squash? What does it ______ like?

2 In the USA Thanksgiving is a very important ______ .

Info box

Before the arrival of the English, the Wampanoag and five other Indian tribes lived in Massachusetts. These were the Massachuset, Pennacook, Nauset, Pocumtuc and Nipmuc.

3 Before Sarah goes to sleep, she says her ______ .

4 When Sarah and Elizabeth milk the goats, they tell each other their ______ .

5 The Pilgrims were ______ when they found an empty Indian village.

6 What ______ the ______ of so many Wampanoag?
Not many people in the Wampanoag villages ______ .

10 REVISION WRITING Mike's e-mail (Expressing personal opinions)

▸ p. 39 • SF (pp. 168–169)

Test

After the trouble in class, Mike was also angry with Gracie and Mrs Tripp. He wrote an e-mail to his cousin. Write his e-mail. Say what happened in class from Mike's point of view and say how he felt about it. These words/phrases will help you:

different opinions • interrupt the lesson • be rude • not my fault • give extra work • do a presentation • I don't think it's fair • in my view • the way I see it • Mrs Tripp/Gracie shouldn't ...

Hi, Sharon!

______

______

______

______

______

______

______

11 REVISION Gracie's dad told her that ... (Indirect speech – statements) ▸ p. 40 • GF 3a (p. 177)

What did Gracie's dad tell her about Plimoth Plantation? Use the reporting verbs **said, told her, explained to/her***.*

1

Plimoth Plantation is a living-history museum, Gracie.

He explained to/told Gracie that Plimoth Plantation was a living-history museum.

2 Dad: It's the best place to find out about Thanksgiving.

3 Dad: You'll be able to talk to the staff.

4 Dad: I've visited Plimoth Plantation twice.

2511

12 Gracie's questions (Indirect speech – questions with question words) ▸ p. 41 • GF 3b (pp. 177–178)

At Plimoth Plantation Gracie asked the colonists lots of questions. What did she ask? Report her questions with **asked** *or* **wanted to know***.*

1 How many English colonists sailed on the Mayflower?

2 When exactly did the Mayflower arrive?

3 How big was the Mayflower?

4 Why do you call yourselves Saints?

5 What is your main food in winter?

6 How long have you been in Plymouth?

7 How many Wampanoag came to the Thanksgiving?

1 Gracie asked *how many English colonists had sailed on the Mayflower.*

2 She wanted to know

3 She asked

4

5

6

2512 7

13 Visitors' questions (Indirect speech – yes/no questions) ► p. 41 • GF 3b (pp. 177–178)

A staff member at the visitor center talks about some funny questions that tourists asked about Plimoth Plantation. How does the staff member report the questions? Begin with **asked** *or* **wanted to know**.

1 Can I buy 17th century food?

One visitor asked *if he could buy 17th century food.*

2 'Can visitors milk the goats?'

One visitor wanted to know ______________________________

3 'Do visitors wear Pilgrim costumes too?'

Another visitor once asked ______________________________

4 'Does the Mayflower II also sail to England and back?'

One person even ______________________________

5 'Will I have to speak to the colonists in 17th century English?'

A woman ______________________________

6 'I'm a good cook. Can I help with the turkey on Thanksgiving Day?'

One man said he was a good cook and ______________________________

2613 ______________________________

14 He told her to ask questions (Indirect speech – commands and requests) ► p. 41 • GF 3c (p. 178)

Report what people at Plimoth Plantation **told**, **asked** *or* **wanted Gracie to do**.

1 Ask the guides lots of questions!

2 Can you show us the way to the Mayflower II, please?

3 Go to the exhibition on the First Thanksgiving.

4 Don't forget the movie!

5 Can you get a booklet for me, please?

1 Gracie's dad told *her to ask the guides lots of questions.*

2 Some tourists ______________________________

3 One guide ______________________________

4 He also ______________________________

2614 5 An old man ______________________________

15 MEDIATION The Wampanoag homesite[1] ▸ p. 41 • SF (p. 165) Track 6

The Müllers want to visit the Wampanoag homesite at Plimoth Plantation. Everybody wants to ask questions, but only son Max speaks English well enough. At the visitor center Max has to mediate. He talks to Jim, one of the guides.

Herr M. Max, frag wie lange der Besuch der Wampanoag homesite dauert. Das möchte ich mir anschauen.

Max Excuse me, how long does it take to visit the Wampanoag homesite, please?

Jim Well, you can look around as long as you like, but you can usually see it in an hour.

Max Er meint, in einer Stunde kann man alles sehen.

Now listen to the CD and continue to mediate for Max.

16 EVERYDAY ENGLISH SPEAKING My visit to Plimoth Plantation ▸ p. 41

Imagine you visited Plimoth Plantation and have to prepare a three-minute talk about it for class. Revise all the information in your student's book and workbook, then make notes or a mind map in your exercise book.

Talk about: the historical background, what you saw, the people you spoke to, some questions you asked, what you liked best and why. The pictures will give you ideas.

My visit to Plimoth Plantation was very interesting and I learned a lot about ... First we ... After that ...

17 STUDY SKILLS Making a handout ▸ p. 42 • SF (p. 160)

a) *What do you know about making a good handout? Read the statements, then tick (✔) the correct boxes.*

1 You give out a handout before your presentation so that listeners can follow it better. ☐

2 You give out a handout after your presentation to remind[2] listeners of what you have said. ☐

3 You must use full sentences for a handout. ☐

4 Your handout must have a title, your name and the date. ☐

5 It isn't important to give sources for the material (articles, books, internet) that you have used. ☐

6 Your handout – like an essay or a report – should have a clear structure. ☐

b) **Extra** *In your exercise book, write down two more statements on how to make a good handout. Then look at Gracie's handout again. Does it help you to follow her presentation? Does it have a clear structure? Write your opinion in a paragraph.*

[1] homesite ['həʊmsaɪt] *Heimstätte* [2] remind [rɪ'maɪnd] *erinnern*

18 READING COURSE
Part 2: The Boston Tea Party (Skimming and scanning) ► p. 42 • SF (pp. 163–164)

a) You have to find out about the Boston Tea Party for homework. Skim the text quickly, then answer b) below.

The Boston Tea Party

December 16, 1773
It was a cold night in Boston. Three English ships (the Dartmouth, the Eleanor and the Beaver) had arrived in Boston Harbour, full of tea from England. But the people of Boston did not want to unload the tea. They were angry with the British Parliament because they had put a high tax[1] on tea to the colonies, which the colonists thought was unfair.

The Tea Act
The British East India Tea company was not doing well, so with the Tea Act the British Parliament put a high tax on tea to the colonies from all other companies. This meant that the colonists could only buy tea from the East India company, as the British wanted. Tea from other companies was now much too expensive for the colonists.

'No taxation without representation'
The British Parliament was over 3000 miles away and the English colonists, who now called themselves Americans, could not speak out against things they thought were wrong or unfair. They were not represented in the British Parliament, but they had to do what King George III and the Parliament wanted. The colonists wanted to be free from Britain.

Protest
The situation made the colonists very angry. They wanted to protest to show the British that they were not happy with the new Tea Act. Some people wanted to fight. Some wanted only a quiet protest. But a group of men, who called themselves 'Sons of Liberty', had decided to take action.

Party time
The Sons of Liberty dressed as Native Americans and climbed onto the three ships. They started to cut open the 342 crates[2] of tea with tomahawks. Then they threw the tea into Boston Harbour, all 45 tons of it. Because they were dressed as Native Americans the British could not blame the colonists. There was no proof, but the British knew that the colonists were responsible[3]. The British became even angrier, and in the end they closed Boston Harbour. Colonists repeated their 'tea party' protests in Maryland, New York and New Jersey in the next few months, and tea was soon boycotted throughout the colonies. The situation got worse.

The Boston Tea Party was an important, symbolic act in the history of America, as it clearly showed that the colonists wanted to be free from Britain. Just two years later Americans were ready to give their lives for their freedom[4], as the first shots fell in Lexington ...

b) Tick (✔) the correct answer. The text is about:

A a celebration. B an exhibition. C an event in history.

c) Now scan the text to find more specific information. Mark the key words in the questions below and look for them when you scan. Underline the information you find while you are scanning.

1 Who was the British king at the time?
2 Why exactly was the Tea Act a problem to the colonists?
3 Explain 'No taxation without representation'.
4 Who were the 'Sons of Liberty'?
5 Why was the Boston Tea Party important ?
6 What came next in the history of America?

Fun fact
Every year on 16th December actors act out the story of the *Boston Tea Party* in Boston Harbor.

[1] tax ['tæks] *Steuer* [2] crate [kreɪt] *Holzkiste*
[3] responsible [rɪ'spɒnsəbl] *verantwortlich* [4] freedom ['friːdəm] *Freiheit*

19 Extra Background File MASSACHUSETTS ▸ pp. 43–44

Test

a) What do you know now about Massachusetts? Do this quiz and find out. Tick (✔) A, B or C. If you are not sure, look at pp. 43–44 of your student's book again. You need the letters in brackets in b).

1 How many British colonies were there in America in 1750?

☐ A 20. (B) ☐ B 15. (C) ☐ C 13. (E)

2 In what year was the Boston Tea Party?

☐ A 1770. (A) ☐ B 1773. (D) ☐ C 1775. (C)

3 The American Declaration of Independence from Britain was in the year …

☐ A 1776. (O) ☐ B 1773. (D) ☐ C 1781. (E)

4 The capital of Massachusetts is …

☐ A Lexington. (P) ☐ B Plymouth. (C) ☐ C Boston. (A)

5 Which university is not in Massachusetts?

☐ A MIT. (O) ☐ B Yale. (P) ☐ C Harvard. (E)

6 What sport do the Boston Red Sox play?

☐ A Ice hockey. (P) ☐ B Basketball. (D) ☐ C Baseball. (C)

7 What is the population of the state of Massachusetts?

☐ A 4.4 million. (E) ☐ B 6.4 million. (C) ☐ C 590,000. (I)

b) Now write the letters in brackets from your answers in a) in the boxes below. If your answers are correct, the letters make the name of a really nice place to spend a summer holiday in Massachusetts. Here are the question numbers:

7	4	5	1		6	3	2

c) What have you learned from the information on pp. 43–44? Write a few sentences on each of these topics:

1 The role of Massachusetts in US history *2* The 'Brain State' *3* Tourism in Massachusetts

1 ____________________

____

____

____

2 ____________________

____

____

____

3 ____________________

____

____

____

20 WORKING WITH THE TEXT I'm going to save my brother ▸ pp. 52–54

a) Understanding the text. In a few sentences, say what each part of the story is about.

1 April, 1775 (ll. 1–79): It's the start of the American Revolution. Sam Meeker

2 February, 1779 (ll. 80–201): Four years later war has destroyed the country. The father

3 1826 (ll. 202–214): 47 years later Tim writes down this story to remember the short life of his brother Sam.

b) Paraphrase these words from the story:

1 soldier: A soldier is a person who

2 prisoner: A prisoner is

3 law:

c) Think carefully about what happens in the story and why. Read the end of the story again. Then finish the statement below. Write your opinion in two or three paragraphs in your exercise book.

'I'm going to save my brother' is a sad story because ...

1 Write the missing words.

1 BC is the ______________________ for 'before Christ'.

2 The Pilgrims' journey on the Mayflower took 66 days ______________ bad weather at sea.

3 I know something really interesting, but I can't tell you because it's a ______________ .

4 How many ______________ members work at Plimoth Plantation?

3101 5 It's rude to ______________ your teacher in class.

2 Complete with the correct verb forms.

1 If Gracie ______________ (not be) rude in class, Mrs Tripp wouldn't have given her extra work.

3102 2 If Gracie hadn't gone to Plimoth Plantation, she ______________ (not find out) the answers to all her questions.

3 Report Gracie's questions.

3103

1 Gracie asked her dad how many times he ______________ to Plimoth Plantation.

2 She wanted to know if the Pilgrims ______________ animals for food.

3 She asked whether visitors ______________ to touch things in the Pilgrims' houses.

4 What did they tell Gracie?

1 Gracie's dad: 'Ask the guides lots of questions.' – He told her ______________ the guides lots of questions.

3104 2 Gracie's mom: 'Don't forget to ask for some booklets.' – She told her ______________ to ask for some booklets.

5 STUDY SKILLS Complete the text.

When you do a presentation, it's a good idea to give your listeners a ______________ . If you give it ______________ the presentation, it will help people to ______________ it better. If you give it after the presentation, listeners will remember it better. At the top you must write your ______________ and the ______________ . You must also give ______________ for material you use.

3105

18 points

Now you

3106 3107 *In your exercise book, write an e-mail to a friend about a museum visit. Remember your writing skills. Write about 150 words. Ideas:*

history teacher • day trip • see a lot of old things • like/not like • interesting

Jetzt kann ich …	Sehr gut!	OK	Verbessern!
HÖREN: Ich kann …			
… längere Texte verstehen, auch wenn ich einige Wörter nicht kenne.	☐	☐	☐
… aus längeren Listenings Details richtig entnehmen.	☐	☐	☐
… den amerikanischen Akzent heraushören.	☐	☐	☐
… mehrere amerikanische Wörter erkennen und verstehen (z.B. *elevator, gas, cellphone, vacation, sidewalk*).	☐	☐	☐
SPRECHEN: Ich kann …			
… meine Meinung zu Themen im Englischunterricht frei äußern, auch wenn ich Fehler mache.	☐	☐	☐
… in einer amerikanischen Stadt nach dem Weg fragen.	☐	☐	☐
… in einem amerikanischen *deli* ohne Probleme bestellen.	☐	☐	☐
… bei einer Besichtigung nach allgemeinen Informationen und nach historischen Fakten fragen.	☐	☐	☐
LESEN: Ich …			
… kann die Texte der Units 1 und 2 lesen und verstehen.	☐	☐	☐
… weiß, wie ich unbekannte Wörter in einem Text erschließen kann.	☐	☐	☐
… kenne die Lesetechniken *skimming* und *scanning* und kann sie anwenden.	☐	☐	☐
… kann Texte über Themen des Alltags und aus der Geschichte lesen und verstehen, auch wenn mir einige Wörter nicht bekannt sind.	☐	☐	☐
SCHREIBEN: Ich …			
… kenne die Texttypen *diary, essay, presentation, handout, blog, e-mail* und *postcard* und kann sie stilistisch unterscheiden.	☐	☐	☐
… kann die britische und die amerikanische Schreibweise unterscheiden (z.B. BE: *colour, centre*; AE: *color, center*).	☐	☐	☐
… kann meine Sätze mit *adjectives, adverbs, time phrases* und *linking words* verbinden und ausbauen, um sie sprachlich interessanter zu gestalten.	☐	☐	☐
LAND UND LEUTE: Ich …			
… kenne die Namen einiger berühmter Sehenswürdigkeiten in New York (z.B. *the Statue of Liberty, Ellis Island, Central Park*).	☐	☐	☐
… könnte mich in Manhattan zurechtfinden. Mehrere Straßennamen sind mir geläufig (z.B. *Fifth Avenue, Broadway, 34th Street*).	☐	☐	☐
… weiß, dass New York fünf Bezirke hat: *Manhattan, Queens, Brooklyn, the Bronx, Staten Island*.	☐	☐	☐
… weiß einiges über *the Empire State Building* und *Ground Zero*.	☐	☐	☐
… habe einiges über die Geschichte New Yorks und Massachusetts gelernt.	☐	☐	☐
… weiß einiges über Plimoth Plantation und die Geschichte der englischen Kolonisten in Amerika.	☐	☐	☐
… weiß etwas über die Wampanoag und den Ursprung von *Thanksgiving*.	☐	☐	☐

Jetzt kann ich ...	Sehr gut!	OK	Verbessern!
GRAMMATIKVERSTÄNDNIS: Ich kann ...			
... das Gerundium (*gerund*) richtig bilden und es als Subjekt oder als Objekt eines Satzes einsetzen (z.B. *Flying is great. / I love flying.*).	☐	☐	☐
... das Gerundium nach gewissen Verben (z.B. *enjoy, finish, miss, practise*) und nach Präpositionen richtig einsetzen (z.B. *I enjoy reading./ I'm interested in learning languages.*).	☐	☐	☐
... mit einem *conditional sentence (type 3)* ausdrücken, was unter bestimmten Bedingungen geschehen wäre oder nicht. Dazu benutze ich im *if*-Satz das *past perfect* und im Hauptsatz *would/could/might have + past participle* (z.B. *If I had lived in London, I would have learnt excellent English.*).	☐	☐	☐
... berichten, was jemand gefragt hat. Dabei benutze ich den *backshift of tenses* (z.B. *'When does the museum open?' → She asked when the museum opened. 'Do you know the answer?' → She asked if/whether I knew the answer.*).	☐	☐	☐
... Aufforderungssätze (*commands*) und Bitten (*requests*) berichten (z.B. *'Ask lots of questions.' → He told me to ask lots of questions. 'Could you help me, please?' → He asked me to help him.*).	☐	☐	☐
VOKABELVERSTÄNDNIS: Ich kann ...			
... amerikanische Wörter von britischen unterscheiden (z.B. BE: *rubbish, lift*; AE: *garbage, elevator*).	☐	☐	☐
... amerikanische Wörter/Wendungen für eine Wegbeschreibung (z.B. *block, downtown, 34th and Broadway*) richtig verwenden.	☐	☐	☐
... Wörter für historische Ereignisse (z.B. *timeline, BC, revolution, colonist, settler, cause, consequence*) richtig verwenden.	☐	☐	☐
SKILLS – LERNEN UND ARBEITEN: Ich ...			
... kenne Arbeitstechniken, die mir helfen, unbekannte Wörter in einem Text ohne Wörterbuch zu erschließen (z.B. Bilder, Überschriften, Kontext, Vor- und Nachsilben).	☐	☐	☐
... kann Gesprochenes auf Englisch oder Deutsch sinngemäß weitergeben (*mediation*), z.B. bei der Einholung von Informationen.	☐	☐	☐

WAS ICH FÜR MEIN ENGLISCHLERNEN GETAN HABE: Ich habe ...	häufig	manchmal	nie
... im Englischunterricht gut aufgepasst und aktiv mitgearbeitet.	☐	☐	☐
... gelernte Arbeitstechniken bewusst eingesetzt.	☐	☐	☐
... die Aufgaben im Grammar File in meinem Buch bearbeitet.	☐	☐	☐

WIE ICH MICH VERBESSERN KÖNNTE: Ich könnte ...

- ... Vokabel- und Grammatikkenntnisse regelmäßig auffrischen. ☐
- ... häufiger ein deutsch-englisches Wörterbuch verwenden. ☐
- ... ausgewählte Workbook-Übungen der Bände 2 und 3 noch einmal bearbeiten. ☐
- ... mir amerikanische Texte von meiner CD anhören, um mich an die Aussprache und Betonung zu gewöhnen. ☐
- ... DVDs auf Englisch anschauen. ☐
- ... englischsprachige Zeitschriften oder Websites lesen. ☐

Unit 3 California, land of dreams

1 What do you know about California? ▸ pp. 56–57

a) Choose two of the pictures 5–11 on pp. 56–57 of your student's book and write a short paragraph about each. Say what each picture shows, and what it tells you about California. You can add information from other sources (TV, internet). Use a German-English dictionary for words you don't know.

Picture ___ : I think picture ___ shows

Picture ___ :

b) Skim pp. 58–63 of your student's book. What do you think you are going to read about in this unit? Write down a few key words. Then wait and see if you were right.

Spanish-speaking workers,

2 WORDS Synonyms ▸ p. 56

a) Match the synonyms in the two lists.

until	equipment	talk about	awful
difficult	woods	terrible	complete
gear	till	continue	be quiet
forest	middle	finish	discuss
centre	find	whether	go on
discover	hard	shut up	if

b) Now mark the word in each sentence that you can change. Then write the synonym in its correct form.

1 We talked about the problems of Native Americans in school today. ▶ discussed

2 Where exactly did they find gold in California? ▶ ______

3 People continued looking for gold for a long time after 1848. ▶ ______

4 How long will it take you to finish your history essay? ▶ ______

5 California is a great place for sports, so you need a lot of sports equipment. ▶ ______

3402 6 Let's ask our teacher if we can go to California on a school trip! ▶ ______

3 WORDS Belonging to an ethnic minority ▸ p. 58

Complete what Luis's friend Akuma says with words from the box.

advantage • attitude • bilingual • disadvantage • discrimination • education • *ethnic minority* • prejudiced • relations • values

Hi! My name is Akuma. My parents are Korean, so we belong to an *ethnic minority*. For me this isn't a ________________ but some Americans are ________________ against immigrants like us. Some kids in our school have problems with ________________ because they look different. A boy I know from India once had a bad time with some white bullies. They said he didn't belong here and he should go home. I think it's a question of ________________. I think that growing up in two cultures is a big ________________. I have American and Korean friends because I speak both languages. I'm ________________ like lots of kids my age. At school ________________ with classmates are good – maybe because I share their ________________. I think a good ________________ is important, and I'm good at baseball. Or maybe it's just because they like my mom's Korean cooking! I wish that all immigrant kids could feel good here, like me.

3503

4 WRITING A help page (Writing a comment to a help page) ▸ p. 58 • SF (pp. 168–169)

Test

This is part of an e-mail that Rabab, a 14-year-old girl from Pakistan, wrote to a teenage help page. Write a comment for the website. Give advice to help her. Write about 100 words in your exercise book.

...
I've lived in California now for five years, but I still feel lonely at school. The girls in my class always talk together in the break, but never to me. It's because I look different and I'm not interested in things they like – make-up or fashion.
They hang out together after school. They go shopping, and do other stuff. They invite each other to their homes, but they never invite me. They do things that I am not allowed to do, like going to discos and parties. They talk about boys all the time of course, but I have never had a boyfriend. My parents want me to grow up in the culture of our home country. What can I do to find friends at school?

– Rabab K., L.A.

You can use these ideas or your own:

- invite the nicest girl to your home, she'll tell the others about you
- offer to help with homework in subjects that you're good at
- tell classmates about your home country and why your family came to the US
- join school clubs that bring you together with others, like a drama group or a dance class
- if things don't get better, talk to your favourite teacher about your problem

Now you

Do you have classmates from other countries? If so, which countries are they from? Have you learnt about their cultures from them?
Or: Are you growing up in two cultures? Are you bilingual? Describe your class situation.

I am German but in my class there are lots of students who are not German. I think it is interesting to learn about different countries and cultures from classmates ...

5 REVISION Earthquake[1] country (Passive – simple past) ▸ p. 58 • GF 4a–b (p. 179)

Complete the text with verbs in the passive – simple past. Read the whole text through first.

Then choose from: call • destroy • hit (2x) • hurt • kill (2x)

Earthquake country: Facts

On April 18, 1906 more than 3,000 people ... in an earthquake and the fires which followed. It ... the Great San Francisco Earthquake. On October 17, 1989 San Francisco's Bay Bridge ... It collapsed. The earthquake lasted[2] only 15 seconds, but 57 people ... and thousands ... badly. On January 17, 1994, at 4.31 in the morning, Los Angeles ... by an earthquake which lasted 40 seconds. 72 people died and hundreds of homes ...

3605

were killed

6 An accident report (Simple past: active and passive) ▸ p. 58 • GF 4a–b (p. 179)

A reporter spoke to the police about a traffic accident in San Clemente. Read his notes and write his report. Be careful: some sentences have to be in the passive.

- corner Main Street/Park Road, 9.30 am
- cyclist ran into old woman
- seen by young woman and boy
- man cycling too fast, couldn't stop
- cycled away, didn't get help
- ambulance called by young woman
- old woman taken to hospital
- description of man given by boy and young woman
- police now looking for man
- description sent to all police stations in San Clemente

At 9.30 am yesterday an accident happened at the corner of Main Street and Park Road. A cyclist ran into an old woman. The accident was seen by a young woman and a boy. The man was cycling too fast and ...

3606

[1] earthquake ['ɜːθkweɪk] *Erdbeben* [2] last [lɑːst] *dauern*

7 Blue box: they ▸ p. 58, p. 208

*Complete with **they**, **them** or **their**.*

Luis Somebody called when you were out, Mom, but __________ didn't give __________ name.

Mom Well, if __________ call again, take __________ number. Just say I'll call __________ back, OK?

8 WORDS Strawberry farming ▸ p. 59

Read the text carefully and write the words in the boxes correctly.

Strawberry farming is important for the state of California. 85% of US strawberries come from there. First, workers prepare the fields with big machines. Then they [tnalp] __________ the strawberries and [yspar] __________ them with insecticides to [ttpreoc] __________ them. Then workers [vrcoe] __________ the plants with [lsptiac] __________. This keeps the [tisnecs] __________ away. [lclgBaooii] __________ methods are also used to protect the plants. When the strawberries are [peri] __________, [grmntai] __________ workers from Mexico [kipc] __________ them and pack them for transportation.

3708

9 What's in the headlines? (Passive – present perfect) ▸ p. 59 • GF 4a–b (p. 179)

Mrs Morales is reading the local newspaper. Luis asks his mom what has happened. Write full sentences in the passive – present perfect. Here are some newspaper headlines:

Youth center closed till summer

New coffee bar opened

Two hurt in motorcycle accident

S.C. High School basketballers beaten again

Main Street bank robbed[1], three arrested[2]

Luis What's in the news, Mom? *Has our school been closed* ? No such luck, I guess!

Mom No, not the school, but the youth center __________ till next summer. Oh, and a new coffee and juice bar __________ in Second Street, so that's good news. You guys will hang out there now, I guess. Let's see what else is new. Oh, the bank on Main Street __________. Two men and a woman __________. And two teenagers __________ in a motorcycle accident. And you won't like this, Luis, but the High School basketball team __________ again.

3709

Fun fact

In 2000, 55 Oscars were stolen on their way to L.A. to the Award[3] Show. 52 were found next to a garbage bin. Willie Fulgear, the man who found them and gave them to the police, got a reward[4] of $50,000 and two tickets to the show. But a few days later a thief broke into his apartment and stole the money!

[1] rob [rɔb] *überfallen, ausrauben* [2] arrest [ə'rest] *verhaften*
[3] award [ə'wɔːd] *Preis* [4] reward [rɪ'wɔːd] *Belohnung*

10 Alcatraz (Passive – modals and will-future)

▸ p. 59 • GF 4c (p. 180)

Complete the text with passive forms. Read the text carefully before you start.

had to/close • couldn't/do • should/buy • may/take • will/remember • can/reach • can/see

Everybody has heard of Alcatraz or of the gang boss Al Capone, who spent four and a half years of his life there.

The prison *had to be closed* in 1963, but now it's a tourist attraction with lots and lots of visitors.

Alcatraz Island ____________ from San Francisco, but it ____________ by ferry only.

Boat tours ____________ at any time during the day, but in the summer months tickets ____________ at least a week before the tour.

Alcatraz ____________ by exciting Hollywood films like *The Rock*. A few prisoners tried to escape from Alcatraz, but it ____________ .

3810

11 What were you shown? (Personal passive)

▸ p. 59 • GF 4d (p. 180)

*Write the sentence parts in **bold** in the passive.*

Luis I once did a tour of a movie studio with my mom. It was a six-hour VIP tour. My uncle Joe works at Universal, so he got us some tickets.

Kim Oh, great. Tell me about it. (1) **What did they show you**?

Luis (2) Well, **they gave us** a tour of the production areas. (3) **They showed us** some cool movie sets[1] from famous movies – like *King Kong* and stuff. Then (4) **they showed us** some special effects, how it's done. It was awesome. Of course I asked lots of questions and (5) **they gave me** some cool information. The tour guide said (6) **they might even offer me** a job after school if I'm good with computers.

Kim Why not? Maybe (7) **they pay special effects people good money**. What else happened?

Luis (8) Well, **they told us** some funny stories about movie actors too, like stuff that went wrong on camera. (9) Oh! And **they gave me** an Oscar – well, to hold, because (10) **they showed us** an Oscar close-up.

1 *What were you shown?*
2 *We were given ...*
3 ____________
4 ____________
5 ____________
6 ____________
7 ____________
8 ____________
9 ____________
10 ____________

3811

[1] set [set] *Schauplatz*

12 READING COURSE
Part 3: US students and sports (Finding the main ideas of a text) ▸ p. 59 • SF (pp. 163–164)

a) *Read the report carefully. Look for the main ideas and examples which support them.*

US high school students: sport – no, thank you!

(1) The state of California offers a wide variety of water and beach sports, together with all other outdoor sports. On average[1], however, US teenagers nationwide do not do enough sport to keep fit and healthy. As children grow older, they become less and less active, and by 12th grade physical[2] activity has reached its lowest level[3].

(2) Experts agree that students in grades 9–12 spend too much time sitting and spend too little time on physical activities. For example, 35% of US high school students do not take part in sports regularly. This fact alone can be the cause of serious[4] health problems in adult life.

(3) One problem is that our modern lifestyle with its electronic media means that teenagers spend too many hours on activities where they just sit. These activities are, for example, watching TV or DVDs, playing video and computer games or using computer and cellphones to contact friends. Studies have shown that 17% of young people in the US watch TV for up to five hours a day, much longer than most working adults.

(4) How students get to school is another cause of physical inactivity[5]. National transportation studies say that for safety reasons most students are taken to school by bus or by car, even if school is only one mile or less away from home. Older students drive to school in their own cars, so walking or cycling to school is something that most high school students just do not do.

(5) What can be done to change the attitude of teenagers to sport and physical activities? In many parts of the USA communities and local government[6] work together to offer physical activity programs for young people. These programs include many sports but also sponsored environmental[7] work.
But physical activity is voluntary[8], so students will join programs only if they are motivating, enjoyable, close to home and free.

b) *Mark the topic of the text green, the main idea of each paragraph red and examples, reasons or explanations blue.*

c) *Which of the main ideas below (A–E) goes with which paragraph (1–5)?*

A: Students do not often join community physical activity programs. (Paragraph ______)

B: Most high school students do not walk or cycle to school. (Paragraph ______)

C: The use of electronic media makes young people physically inactive. (Paragraph ______)

D: US high school students do not spend enough time doing sports. (Paragraph ______)

E: Experts say that students in grades 9–12 sit too much in their free time. (Paragraph ______)

d) **Extra** *What's the general attitude to sports and health in your school year? Do you and your friends take part in physical activities (running, cycling, swimming, etc.) in your free time? Or do you spend more time with electronic media? Write about 100 words in your exercise book.*

[1] average ['ævərɪdʒ] *Durchschnitt* [2] physical ['fɪzɪkl] *körperlich*
[3] lowest level ['ləʊɪst 'levl] *niedrigstes Niveau* [4] serious ['sɪəriəs] *ernst* [5] inactivity [ˌɪnæk'tɪvəti] *Untätigkeit*
[6] government ['gʌvənmənt] *Regierung* [7] environmental [ɪnˌvaɪrən'mentl] *Umwelt-*
[8] voluntary ['vɒləntri] *freiwillig*

13 The guy reading the magazine (Participle clauses) ▸ p. 60 • GF 5 (p. 181)

Say who the people in the picture are. Describe them with a participle clause.

1 Rick is the guy *reading the magazine.*

2 Josie is the girl ______

3 Matt ______

4 Gina ______

5 Brad ______

4013 6 Ben and Ed ______

14 EVERYDAY ENGLISH SPEAKING Living in California ▸ p. 60

Would you like to live in California? Think of at least three points for and against. Look at the pictures for ideas, write notes, then prepare your arguments for a class discussion.

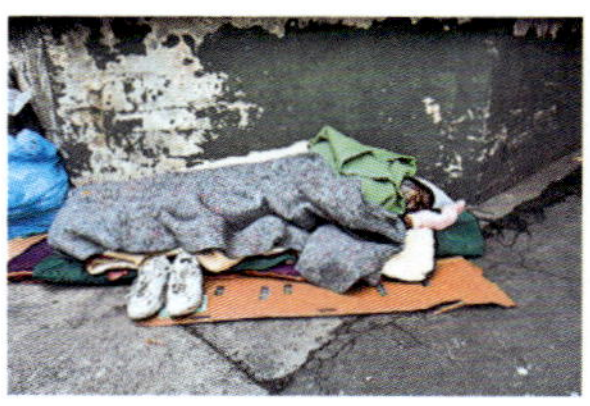

Brainstorm your ideas and make notes first.

Good things:	Bad things:
good weather: sunny and warm all year;	*earthquakes; forest fires;*
beaches:	

15 They want everybody to help (Verb + object + to-infinitive) ▸ p. 61 • GF 6a (p. 182)

*a) The San Clemente Clean Ocean Program is very important. What exactly does it **want/ask/tell/help people to do**? Make sentences with infinitive constructions.*

1 It helps – people – protect the environment

It helps people to protect the environment.

2 It wants – homeowners and visitors – prevent pollution of the ocean

____

____

3 It wants – everybody – keep the beaches clean

____

4 It tells – people – leave less rubbish on the beaches

____

5 It wants – homeowners – pay just 16 cents a day

____

6 It would like – people of all ages – support the program

____

4115

b) Find information about international organizations, for example, Greenpeace, Friends of the Earth. What do they want people to do? In your exercise book, write a few sentences with infinitive constructions about their general and/or specific aims.

International organizations want people/everybody/the public to support them/to become members. They want the public/everybody to find out about environmental problems worldwide ...

16 At the tourist information center (Question word + to-infinitive) ▸ p. 61 • GF 6b (p. 182)

In San Francisco you asked lots of questions at the tourist information center. What did they tell you?

*a) Complete the sentences with a question word + **to**-infinitive.*

1 They told us *where to stay.* (stay)

2 ... *which* _______________ (sights/visit)

3 ... _______________ (eat)

4 ... _______________ (get/Chinatown)

5 ... _______________ (tours/take)

6 ... _______________ (do in the evenings)

*b) **Extra** Now complete the sentences with an infinitive construction and your own ideas.*

1 They also told us the best place *to buy tour tickets.*

2 ... the cheapest way _______________

____

3 ... the best time _______________

____

4 ... the easiest way _______________

____

17 LISTENING A dream that came true ▸ p. 61 • SF (p. 161) Track 7

Luis had to find out some facts about the Golden Gate Bridge for homework, but he made his notes in a hurry and wrote down some wrong details. Listen and correct Luis's mistakes.

1 The bridge is ~~0.7~~ miles long. 1.7

2 It takes about 30 minutes to walk across the bridge. ______

3 Joseph Strauss' father was an engineer. ______

4 Strauss started to build the bridge in 1934. ______

5 It was opened on June 20th at 12 o'clock midday. ______

6 It cost 25 million dollars to build. ______

7 It's foggy near the bridge from April to June. ______

8 The bridge is painted gold. ______

9 28 painters work on the bridge. ______

10 Strauss died 10 years after the bridge was finished. ______

18 STUDY SKILLS Outlining ▸ p. 61 • SF (p. 159)

a) *Right or wrong? What do you know about outlining? Tick (✓) the correct sentences.*

An outline ...

- helps you to organize and structure your ideas before you write. ☑
- helps you to find the main ideas for research. ☐
- should be written in full sentences. ☐
- should include main ideas, then sub-points of this idea. ☐
- should include details of statistics, pictures, etc. ☐
- should include examples and reasons/explanations. ☐

b) *In your exercise book, write an outline for a short text about the Californian Gold Rush. Before you start, it's a good idea to brainstorm your ideas.*

Here are some points which you could research and include. You can finish the outline here or make your own outline with different points:

when and where gold was first found • who found it • what the consequences were • going west • who the 'forty-niners' (49s) were • where the men/families came from • how many people went west to look for gold • effects on Native Americans • how much gold was found • how many years the Gold Rush went on • effects of the Gold Rush on California's population • meaning of the Gold Rush for the state today

The Californian Gold Rush

OUTLINE	NOTES
I. Background history	James Marshall
A. who found gold	
B. ______	______
	______
II. Consequences	
A. Going west ...	______
1. who: 'forty-niners'	______
2. how: ______	______
______	______
B. Native Americans	

19 Extra Background File WELCOME TO CALIFORNIA! ▸ pp. 62–63

Test

a) What do you know about California? Tick (✔) A, B or C. You need the letters in brackets in b).

1 California became the 31st state of the USA in …

A 1846. (S)	B 1848. (A)	C 1850. (E)

2 'Silicon Valley' is the home of …

A the movie industry. (E)	B the computer industry. (S)	C fruit and vegetable farming. (A)

3 Hollywood is part of …

A San Francisco. (G)	B San Diego. (E)	C Los Angeles. (N)

4 The first Hollywood movie was made in …

A 1850. (D)	B 1906. (E)	C 1911. (I)

5 You can take a ride on a cable car through the streets of …

A San Francisco. (Y)	B Los Angeles. (R)	C San Clemente. (T)

6 What are sequoias?

A Mexican food. (N)	B A kind of Californian fruit. (I)	C Big trees. (D)

b) Now write the letters in brackets from a) in the boxes below. If your answers are correct, the letters make a famous Hollywood name. Here are the question numbers:

6	4	2	3	1	5

c) What have you learnt from the information on pp. 62–63 in your student's book? Write two interesting facts about each of these topics:

1 Industry in California 2 Hollywood 3 San Francisco 4 Earthquake country

1

2

3

4

20 WORKING WITH THE TEXT The circuit ▸ pp. 72–74

a) Read pp. 72–74 of your student's book again, then put these events in the correct order. Write numbers.

1 Their new home is an old garage. ____

2 Panchito gets on the school bus for the first time that year. ____

3 Panchito feels sick during the work because it's very hot. ____

4 The family moves to Fresno. *1*

5 When Panchito gets home, he sees that the boxes are packed again. ____

6 Panchito gets up very early because he can't sleep. ____

7 Roberto is sad because he can't go to school. ____

8 When the school bus arrives Panchito and Roberto hide. ____

9 Papá and Roberto leave to go to work in the cotton fields. ____

10 Mr Lema is understanding and wants to help Panchito. ____

b) What does the story tell you about Panchito's family? Scan pp. 72–74, make notes and write about 80 words. The following words will help you: ***large family • illegal migrant workers from Mexico • move from place to place on 'the circuit' • little or no school for children • very hard work for little money • poor, bad housing • future***

c) **Extra** *Outline the problems of the state of California and its illegal migrant workers. How do you think this problem could be solved[1]? Use other information you have learnt about migrant workers in this unit too. Make notes first, then write about 80 words in your exercise book.*

[1] solve [sɒlv] *lösen*

1 Write the missing words.

1 If you grow up with two languages and speak both, you are ______________.

2 If you go to another country to work and live without papers, you are an ______________ immigrant.

3 The way you think or feel about someone or something is called your '______________'.

4 I think being ______________ against immigrants is wrong.

5 To get a good job you need a good school ______________.

4501 *6* Being able to speak more than one language is an ______________ when you want to get a job.

2 Complete the word families.

	Verb	Noun	Adjective
1	–	wealth	
2	think		–
3	–	environment	
4		success	successful
5	discriminate		–
6	warn		–

4502

3 What does she want them to do?

1 Mrs Morales wants ______________

4503 *2* She'd like ______________

4 Write the sentences in the personal passive.

1 They showed Luis round the movie studios. ______________

2 They gave the people on the tour lots of information.

4504 ______________

5 Describe the twins Gina and Fay using a participle clause.

1 The twin ______________ is Gina.

4505 *2* And the twin ______________ is Fay – I think.

18 points

Now you

4506 4507 *Write a short essay with the title 'California – a dreamland?' Write a paragraph each on* ***industry, tourist activities*** *and* ***problems of the state****. Remember to use a topic sentence and your writing skills. Write about 150 words in your exercise book.*

Unit 4 Hermann says 'Willkommen'

1 Hermann and the Schmidts

▸ pp. 76–77

Test

a) What do you know about Hermann and the Schmidts? Look at pp. 76–77 of your student's book again. Have you listened to 'The Krugers and the Schmidts' in your student's book? If yes, mark a number.

	Right	Wrong
1 The Schmidts arrive at St. Louis international airport.	15	45
2 The journey by car from St. Louis to Hermann only takes half an hour.	65	15
3 The Schmidts are going to Hermann for a summer holiday.	15	20
4 Hermann lies south of Interstate 70.	30	28
5 Hermann is on the Missouri River.	44	38
6 The small town has a population of 3,674.	36	26
7 There aren't many restaurants in Hermann.	75	90
8 Lots of tourists visit Hermann in summer.	95	44
9 Timo and Anna will go to the same school.	22	30
4601 10 Timo and Jake will go to the same school.	35	22

b) Now add together the numbers that are marked: ______.

If your answers are correct, you have written the number of students at Hermann High School. Check your answer on p. 77 of your student's book.

c) Look at the photos of Hermann on pp. 76–77. Write a description of the town in about 80 words. Use topic sentences and paragraphs.

Hermann is a small town in the state of Missouri. Farmers grow grapes in the area, so the main industry

d) Compare Hermann High School (photo D in your student's book) with your school. Is your school modern too? Has your school got 400 students or more? Has your school got a running track, a football pitch and equipment for athletics? Has your school got a large car park? Write 80–100 words in your exercise book.

Our school is modern too. / Our school isn't as modern as … Our school looks quite different from …

2 WORDS All about … American schools ► p. 78

a) Draw lines to match the information in the boxes.

US school system

Ages 6–11	High School	Grades 1–5
Ages 11–14	Elementary School	Grades 9–12
Ages 14–18	Middle School	Grades 6–8

US school grades

A	below average
B	failure
C	excellent
D	good
F	average

b) If you went to school in the USA, which school would you go to? Which grade would you be in? What about your brothers and sisters?

I'd go to

c) Which US grades would you have in your main subjects?

I think I'd have a B in English and a

3 WORDS School words: BE and AE ► p. 78

a) Complete the lists.

1 Schulstunde — period — lesson

2 Jahrgangsstufe

3 Anschlagtafel

4 Sommerferien

5 Stundenplan

6 Schulnote

b) Where are the two students from?

I'm in year 9. Our timetable is good this year. I've just read our sports results on the notice board. My next lesson is PE in the gym.

My schedule is OK and my grades aren't too bad, but I'm looking forward to the summer vacation.

4703

Cathy is from the ____________.

Josh ____________.

4 EVERYDAY ENGLISH SPEAKING A talk about schools ▸ p. 78

Timo has to tell his new class about school in Germany. He wants to talk about the main differences between US and German schools. Here are his notes:

	Germany	USA
1 grades:	1–6	A–F
2 school day:	not usually afternoon	until 3 pm every day
3 lunch:	usually no lunch	hot lunch at school ☺ ☺
4 rooms:	class has own classroom for subjects, teachers mostly come to class	different rooms for different subjects, class has to change rooms between periods
5 vacation:	6 weeks in summer	3 months in summer ☺ ☺ ☺
6 extracurriculars:	not many	a lot – very important ☺
7 school bus:	not usual	usual ☺

Prepare a talk from Timo's notes and practise it for class. Make notes in your exercise book.

German schools are different from US schools in a few ways. For example, school grades are different, the school day and extracurricular activities. First I want to talk about ...

Extra Now you

What do you think is good about American schools? Say why. What do you like better at your German school? Write two paragraphs in your exercise book.

Some things about American schools are really good. For example, the long summer holidays and ...

5 Blue box: Beginning and ending letters ▸ p. 78, p. 215

Correct the mistakes.

1 When you write a formal letter in BE to someone you don't know, you end with 'All the best'.

Wrong. You end with 'Yours faithfully'.

2 When you write to good friends or family in BE or AE, you end with 'Yours sincerely'.

3 When you write a formal letter in BE and you know the person's name, you end with 'Best wishes'.

4 When you write a formal letter in BE and you don't know the person's name, you end with 'Yours truly'.

5 When you write a formal letter in BE to someone you don't know, you start with 'Dear Mr or Mrs ...'

6 WRITING A letter to a magazine

▸ p. 78 • SF (p. 169)

a) Complete the text.

When you write to a magazine you can start your letter with '______________' or 'Dear ...' and the name of the mag. People usually write to magazines to give their ______________ about an article, or to agree or disagree with someone's comment. But if you give your opinion, you should also give ______________ for your opinion. You can end your letter with 'Yours', 'Sincerely', or '________________________'.

Test

b) In your exercise book, write a letter to a magazine called 'Sixteen'. Write your opinion about German schools. What do you think is good and bad? For example, should the summer holidays be longer? What would you change if you could?

Dear Sixteen,

There are a few things about German schools that I would like to change if I could. For example, I don't like ...

There are some good things too. For example, ...

7 LISTENING Facts and figures

▸ p. 79 • SF (p. 161) Track 8

Test

Listen carefully to the information about Hermann, St. Louis and Missouri and fill in the chart.

	Hermann	St. Louis	Missouri
Founded in	*1837*		
Population			
Area			
German families			
Students at Hermann High			
9th grade students			
Girl students			
Average temperature (summer)			
Hottest temperature			
Average temperature (winter)			
Coldest temperature			
Largest ethnic group			

8 Jake's German barbecue[1] (Countable and uncountable nouns) ▸ p. 79 • GF 7a–b (p. 183)

Complete the text with: some • much • many

Jake hasn't got *much* pocket money, but he'd like to have a German barbecue for Timo and Anna and his friends. But before he starts his plans, he has to ask himself ________ questions. How ________ kids should he invite? How ________ money can he spend? How ________ food should he buy? Maybe his mom will give him ________ help. He'll need ________ sausages, but how ________ sausages will the kids eat? And ________ potato salad, but how ________ should he make? He'll need ________ barbecue sauce, but how ________ bottles? And very important, he'll need ________ great music.

Fun fact

St. Louis is the home of the soda 7Up, and in St. Louis more barbecue sauce is eaten than in any other American city!

5111

9 Blue box: little ('wenig') – few ('wenige') ▸ p. 79, p. 214 • GF 7c (p. 184)

a) Complete with a little, a few, little, less, (the) least.

1 You should eat very *little* red meat and butter, and it's a good idea to eat ________ white bread and pasta too.
2 Jake has to go shopping. There's only ________ milk and ________ strawberries in the fridge.
3 Jake is having a snack, ________ sandwiches and ________ fruit salad.
4 Anna saves ________ pocket money every week, about twelve dollars. Timo saves ________ money than Anna, maybe five to ten dollars. But Jake saves ________ money, usually nothing!

b) Compare yourself with friends/your family. Write sentences with a little, less, (the) least.

1 How much fast food do you eat? *I eat* ________
2 How much time do you spend on hobbies? ________
____
3 How much money do you save? ________
____

5009

Info box

Missouri ...
- is the birthplace of 33rd US President Harry S. Truman, Jesse James (outlaw[2]) and Mark Twain, author of *Tom Sawyer and The Adventures of Huckleberry Finn*.
- is the home of the world's tallest monument, the Gateway Arch[3] in St. Louis.
- is the birthplace of peanut[4] butter and the ice cream cone[5].

[1] barbecue ['bɑːbɪkjuː] *Grillfest* [2] outlaw ['aʊtlɔː] *Bandit*
[3] arch [ɑːtʃ] *Bogen* [4] peanut ['piːnʌt] *Erdnuss* [5] cone [kəʊn] *Spitztüte*

10 WORDS Word building (Nouns from verbs and adjectives) ▸ p. 79

a) *Which verb or adjective do these nouns come from? If you are not sure, use your dictionary.*

activity	– *active*	discrimination	– ______	discussion	– ______
fitness	– ______	madness	– ______	installation	– ______
nationality	– ______	nervousness	– ______	presentation	– ______
revision	– ______	translation	– ______	weakness	– ______

b) *Now complete the sentences with a noun from a).*

1 Timo loves football, so good health and ______ are important to him.

2 There's a Science test next week, so the students have to do some ______ at the weekend.

3 Timo thinks that showing hogs is a very strange ______, but he's going to join the FFA.

4 At the FFA meeting there was a good ______ on the Missouri wine industry.

5 Mr Kruger speaks American English and German. Which ______ is he? American or German?

11 WORDS Opposites ▸ p. 80

a) *Fill in the opposites.*

soft	– *hard*	prefix	– ______	synonym	– ______
majority	– ______	a lot	– ______	the most	– ______
appear	– ______	advantage	– ______	above	– ______
5008 legal	– ______	dead	– ______	possible	– ______

b) *Choose five pairs from a) and write five sentences in your exercise book. Use a pair in each sentence.*

My bed is soft, but the beds in the youth hostel were hard.

12 School is different in Hermann (The definite article) ▸ p. 80 • GF 8 (p. 185)

Add **the** *where you need it.*

1 *The* school that Anna goes to in Hermann is a middle school. She likes it. She says '______ school is fun!'

2 ______ subjects that Timo has now are not all the same as ______ subjects he had in Bad Arolsen.

3 ______ sports teams in Germany don't have cheerleaders, but ______ sports teams at Hermann High all have cheerleaders.

4 Timo likes ______ hamburgers at the school cafeteria, although ______ hamburgers aren't his favourite food.

5112 5 ______ homework isn't usually a problem for Timo, but ______ homework that he does in the school bus is often wrong.

13 READING COURSE Part 4: Summer jobs in the US (Careful reading) ▸ p. 80 • SF 7 (p. 164)

a) Read the magazine article carefully to understand the main facts.

When summer comes, for most teens it means lots of free time, in the US usually from June to August. Some students go to summer camps or go on vacation with family. The ones who stay at home often take part in organized sports programmes or just hang out with friends. But many teens need money, for their families and for themselves, so they try to organize a job for the summer vacation. (1)

What kind of summer vacation jobs do teens do?
Younger teens look for jobs in their hometowns. About 25% have jobs in restaurants, about 25% help out in shops, 11% have an office job[1]. The rest do garden work or deliver pizzas. Some work at petrol stations and wash cars. (2)

We looked at statistics and found out that now there are fewer summer jobs available to teen workers than in past years. Why is this?
We spoke to high school students in three US states. Here are some of their comments:
Matt B., 16, from Germantown, Tennessee said: 'I have a part-time job in a supermarket during the school year and I'm looking for a summer job too. I want to work because I need the money for college later. The problem is that there aren't many jobs for teens. Adults who have lost their jobs and seniors who need money are also looking for low-paid[2] work, so they get the jobs.' (3)

15-year-old Carol S. from San José, California said: 'There are lots of summer jobs here because of all the tourists. My sister is 18. She has work experience and she's at university, so she can work for longer than three months in summer. She has no problem getting a job, but it's more difficult for me.' (4)

'A lot of kids in my grade apply for a summer workplace, but mostly without success. Kids our age only get boring jobs and not much money. Some employers[3] think that older people have a more dependable attitude at the workplace. Some have the view that teenagers want money but are not really prepared to work hard for it. But we have to start somewhere. We need early work experience,' said 15-year-old Guy C. from Missouri City, Texas, 'but sometimes it's hard to get.' (5)

b) In which paragraphs does the text give direct information about the following? Write the paragraph number.

- how much summer vacation high school students have: Paragraph ____
- how high school students spend the summer vacation: Paragraph ____
- what kind of work high school students do: Paragraph ____

c) The text says that there are fewer summer jobs for high school students than a few years ago. Why is this? Find facts in the text which explain the reasons, and write the line number. Then draw a conclusion about the reasons.

____

____

____

● *d)* **Extra** *If you were a high school student in the States, would you try to get a summer vacation job? What kind of work would you like to do? Write a paragraph in your exercise book.*

[1] office job ['ɒfɪs] *Büroarbeit* [2] low-paid [ləʊ] *schlecht bezahlt* [3] employer [ɪm'plɔɪə(r)] *Arbeitgeber/in*

14 Hermann celebrates (Prepositions) ▸ p. 81

Underline the correct preposition in brackets.

1 Many tourists (out of/of/from) Germany travel to Missouri to take part (on/in/at) Hermann's festivals, which take place (to/at/in) different times (throughout/through) the year.

2 Hermann is the 'sausage capital (of/in/from) Missouri', and the first festival (in/of/from) the year is the Wurstfest (in/on) March.

3 Maifest is always(at/in/on) the third weekend in May. The first Maifest took place (in/at) 1870.

4 Oktoberfest is held (on/in/at) the four weekends in October.

5 People who are not interested (for/in/on) crowded festivals can enjoy the beautiful scenery. For example, you can tour Missouri's wine country (on/by/with) bike and visit the wineries. You can also visit some of the 150 historic homes and buildings (of/out of/from) the 1870s.

5314 6 Hermann is known (for/about) its friendly atmosphere[1] and love (of/for/in) traditions. Come and see!

15 REVISION They wanted to know ... (Infinitive constructions) ▸ p. 81 • GF 6b (p. 182)

It's Maifest in Hermann. Some young tourists have just arrived. They ask Jake questions. Write sentences with a question word + to-Infinitiv.

1 What happens at Maifest?
What can we expect?

1 They wanted to know *what to expect at Maifest.*

2 'Where should we stay? Where is it good – and cheap.'

They didn't know *where* ____________________

3 'What events will there be? Who can we ask?'

Jake told them ____________________ about Maifest events.

4 'Where can we get a Maifest programme?'

They wanted to know ____________________ a Maifest programme.

5 'And what special kinds of German food should we eat?'

They didn't know ____________________

6 'What should we see while we're here? Historic buildings? Wineries?'

Jake told them ____________________

7 'How long should we stay? Just a day or a whole weekend?'

They didn't know ____________________

[1] atmosphere ['ætməsfɪə(r)]

16 STUDY SKILLS Summary writing: Hermann Maifest

▸ p. 81 • SF (p. 167)

Test

a) Read the story about Dylan and his friends at Maifest in Hermann. Look for the main events.

It was the third weekend in May, Maifest time. The whole of Hermann was excited. The town was alive with attractions, shows, singing and dancing.

'Now be sure to have a good time, you guys, and take care of Bobby, Dylan. Don't lose him. There will be so many visitors in town this weekend, ' said Mrs Kaiser, as Dylan, Donna and Mike left for the Maifest.
The three students were part of the High School band, so they were already dressed in their German costumes. Dylan even had a solo part on his trumpet. Nobody could play the trumpet like Dylan.

'I just love Maifest', Donna said as they walked through the busy streets in the sunshine. 'Why can't we have Maifest every weekend? There's so much to see, and lots of cute[1] guys come from other high schools!'

'Girls!' said Dylan, as they turned into Schiller Street. They stopped to listen to the Spitzbaum German Band, then they looked at the food stalls[2] and the big market at Volksplatz. Bobby loved the puppet[3] show and the mini train ride. Then they met more friends, laughed, joked and cheered.

An hour later Dylan looked at his watch. It would soon be time for their concert.
'I have to take Bobby home first, then I'll meet you guys later in the Festhalle, OK? Come on, Bobby, we have to go home now. Bobby? Bobby? Where is he? Where's Bobby?' Bobby wasn't there ...

Dylan, Donna and the others looked everywhere, but Bobby was nowhere. They asked lots of people on the streets, but nobody had seen him. Maifest was no fun any more. Dylan was scared, really scared. Had someone taken his little brother?

'Dylan, I think you should call your mom,' said Donna in a nervous voice.
'But Mom will kill me, Donna. She told me to look after Bobby – but I didn't. I was just too busy having fun with you guys. And what about our concert? I have to play my trumpet solo in ten minutes! Bobby must be somewhere. We just have to look everywhere again – fast.'

'Hey, look! Here comes the parade! Look at the costumes! It's just like the very first Maifest in the 1870s,' said Mike. But nobody was listening ...

'Call your mom, Dylan. You have to call her,' said Donna again. Nervously, Dylan took his cellphone out of his pocket ...

'Hey, guys, look at the old German cars in the parade, and the old fire truck[4] and ... Dylan, look who's sitting in the old fire truck with my dad, wearing a fire helmet – it's Bobby!'

'Oh, Mom! Hi, Mom! Er ... it's Dylan. I just wanted to tell you that we're having a great time – Bobby too.'

b) Underline the sentences which tell you the main events or important facts. Then write notes in your exercise book.

c) Write a summary of the story in your own words. Remember to leave out direct speech, details and description, and use the simple present. Write about 100 words.

The story is about Dylan, a student from Hermann High School, who goes to Maifest with his friends and his little brother. First they ...,

[1] cute [kjuːt] *süß, hübsch* [2] stall [stɔːl] *Stand, Bude*
[3] puppet ['pʌpɪt] *Marionette, Puppe* [4] fire truck [trʌk] *Feuerwehrauto*

17 Extra Background File GOING WEST ▸ pp. 82–83

a) Read the statements. Are they right or wrong? Mark a letter.

	Right	Wrong
1 Hermann was founded in 1837.	I	S
2 When World War I started, the people of Hermann stopped speaking German.	N	T
3 The first states of the United States were in the West.	L	D
4 Missouri became a state in 1840.	O	E
5 After 1848 Missouri became the 'Gateway to the West'.	P	I
6 Wagon trains were the safest way to travel to the West.	E	C
7 People bought all the things they needed for the long journey in Hermann.	B	N
8 More than half a million people travelled west with the wagon trains.	D	P
9 The first railway across the country was finished in 1869.	E	A
10 About ten per cent were killed by wild animals or Native Americans.	S	N
11 A few Native Americans died from illnesses the European settlers brought.	R	C
12 Today only 1.5% of the US population are Native Americans.	E	T

If your answers are correct, the letters give you the name of a town in Missouri: __________

b) Answer the questions in one or two sentences each.

A: Why was the town of Hermann founded?

B: Why did so many people want to go west in the years after 1848? Write two reasons.

C: Why was the journey west so hard?

D: What happened to the Native Americans when the settlers went west?

18 WORKING WITH THE TEXT Angus Bethune's moment ▸ pp. 90–92

a) *Finish the statements with information from the story.*

1 The story is about a boy called Angus who *has problems at school because he's big.*

2 Angus is elected Winter Ball King, but ______

3 Angus was elected because Melissa's boyfriend, Rick, ______

4 Angus is OK on the dance floor because ______

5 Melissa tells Angus that ______

6 After the first dance ______

7 When Angus and Melissa dance the second time, ______

8 At the end Rick is angry with Melissa because he thinks ______

9 Angus shows Rick his fist because ______

10 Angus is happy because ______

b) *Choose one picture and describe what is happening.*

Picture ... shows the scene where ______

c) *Do you like the ending? Why or why not? Write a short paragraph.*

Ideas: *funny • surprising • fantastic • clever • unrealistic • sad • silly*

I like the ending. In my opinion it's ... because ... I don't think the ending is very realistic because ...

d) *What are the advantages and disadvantages of 1) looking good and acting cool like Rick and 2) being a really nice person like Angus? In your exercise book, write your opinion in a paragraph.*

1 Write the missing words.

1 ________________ is one of Hermann's main industries.

2 Your ________________ are the people who lived a long time before you.

3 US students do lots of ________________ activities after school.

4 Jake: 'Being in the FFA will look good when I ________________ college or my first job.'

5 Timo has a new subject: American History and ________________ .

5701 6 In the US students in grades 1–5 (ages 6–11) go to ________________ school.

2 Underline the correct word or phrase.

1 Timo has only got (a little/a few) homework today, but he needs (a lot of/many) information about Hermann's wineries for an essay. His dad told him (a few/a little) important facts.

5702 2 Anna saves a little money, Timo saves (less/a few) and Jake saves (fewer/the least).

3 Add the where you need it.

1 Jake: I need some money for the weekend. I'm visiting a friend in St. Louis.

The problem is, I've already spent ________ money I got for my birthday.

Timo: I know what you mean. ______ money is only a problem when you don't have any.

2 ______ tourists always come to Hermann at Maifest and Oktoberfest time. Lots of them are from

5703 Germany. ________ tourists who took part in the Maifest parade were from Rüdesheim.

4 STUDY SKILLS Summary writing: Find and tick (✓) the five correct statements.

To write a good summary you should ...

- give only the most important information from the original text. ______
- tell the reader what the text or story is about in the first few sentences. ______
- explain **who** does **what**, **where**, **when** and **why**. ______
- give lots of details. ______
- use the simple present and your own words. ______
- leave out examples and direct speech. ______
- 5704 use lots of adjectives for description and comparisons. ______

20 points

Now you

5705
5706 *Write a text with the title 'US and German schools: a comparison'. Use the information in your student's book and exercises 2–4 of this unit in your workbook. Remember your writing skills. Write about 120 words in your exercise book.*

Here are some exercises that will help you with your practice test 2.

1 WORDS Holidays ▸ pp. 94–95

a) Match the words in the box to the kind of holiday. Make three lists.

art galleries • *ball games* • bay • *binoculars* • cabin • camping gear • caravan • cathedral • church • column • cows • downtown • exhibition • frisbee • goats • gorge • hike • lake • market • mosque • museum • ocean • palace • parliament • path • rocks • sea • sunglasses • suntan • surfboard • swimming trunks • swimsuit • tent • ticket office • tour guide • towel • tower • trail • valley • views • visibility • volleyball • walking shoes • waves • wildlife

A mountain holiday: *binoculars,* ______

______

A beach holiday: *ball games,* ______

______

A sightseeing holiday: *art galleries,* ______

______

b) Which kind of holiday from a) do you like best? Write your reasons in a paragraph.

I like ______

______

______

______

______

2 Going on holiday (Mixed prepositions) ▸ pp. 94–95

Complete with the correct prepositions: ***of • at • in • on • to • by***

1 We usually go *on* holiday ______ summer.

2 When you flew ______ New York, did you land ______ JFK? It's ______ Queens, isn't it?

3 When it's 10 o'clock ______ the morning in New York, it's 4 o'clock ______ the afternoon in Germany.

4 I've taken a really good photo ______ the Golden Gate Bridge. I'll show it ______ you tomorrow.

5 My dad doesn't like flying. He goes everywhere ______ train or car.

6 My mum doesn't like sitting ______ the beach all day. She prefers going ______ a boat trip or a bus tour.

3 My dream holiday (Conditional sentences 2) ▸ pp. 94–95 • GF 2b (p. 175) • Revision 11 (p. 77)

Where would you spend your US dream holiday – if you could?
Grand Canyon, New York, San Francisco, Las Vegas, Los Angeles, Miami, Washington?
Choose a place. If you **went** *there, what* **would/could** *you* **do**? *Write a paragraph.*

I would spend my US dream holiday in ... if I could. I would go to ... If I went there, I could ...

____

____

____

____

____

____

____

____

4 SPEAKING Making suggestions, agreeing or disagreeing ▸ pp. 94–95

a) *How would you make a suggestion? How would you agree or disagree with a suggestion? Complete the phrases.*

Making suggestions	Let's *go / watch / ...* ______
	We ______
	What ______
Agreeing	That's ______
	Yes, let's ______
Disagreeing	I don't really ______
	I'm not ______

b) *Look at the photos of the beach and the aqua park. A friend suggests going to one of these places. What would you say? Give your reasons. Write a dialoge in your exercise book.*

Jetzt kann ich ...	Sehr gut!	OK	Verbessern!
HÖREN: Ich kann ...			
... längere Texte und Dialoge verstehen, auch wenn ich einige Wörter nicht kenne.	☐	☐	☐
... aus Listenings (z.B. Durchsagen) Details richtig heraushören.	☐	☐	☐
... den Akzent britischer und amerikanischer Sprecher/innen heraushören.	☐	☐	☐
SPRECHEN: Ich kann ...			
... anhand von Bildern eine Stadt und ihre Umgebung beschreiben.	☐	☐	☐
... meine Meinung zu Themen (z.B. Probleme von Migranten in Kalifornien, Unterschiede zwischen deutschen und amerikanischen Schulen) frei äußern.	☐	☐	☐
LESEN: Ich kann ...			
... die Hauptaussagen (*main ideas*), Beispiele (*examples*) und Begründungen (*reasons*) in einem Sachtext erkennen.	☐	☐	☐
... in einem Sachtext Schlussfolgerungen aus gesammelten Fakten ziehen, wobei sich die Fakten an verschiedenen Stellen im Text befinden können.	☐	☐	☐
... eine *timeline* geschichtlicher Ereignisse richtig verstehen.	☐	☐	☐
... die Texte der Units 3 und 4 lesen und verstehen.	☐	☐	☐
SCHREIBEN: Ich kann ...			
... einen *comment* für eine Website schreiben.	☐	☐	☐
... eine *summary* schreiben, indem ich die Hauptereignisse und das Wichtigste zu den 5 Ws eines Textes mit eigenen Worten wiedergebe. Detaillierte Beschreibungen und direkte Rede lasse ich weg.	☐	☐	☐
... einen Brief an eine amerikanische oder britische Zeitschrift schreiben. Dabei benutze ich die entsprechende Anrede und beende meinen Brief mit der passenden Grußformel.	☐	☐	☐
LAND UND LEUTE: Ich ...			
... habe Einblicke in die Situation von Einwanderern in den USA gewonnen.	☐	☐	☐
... weiß vieles über das Leben an einer amerikanischen High School (z.B. typische Fächer, das Notensystem A–F).	☐	☐	☐
... weiß, was *extracurricular activities* sind und dass sie an US High Schools wichtig sind.	☐	☐	☐
... habe einiges über die US Staaten Kalifornien und Missouri gelernt (z.B. Bevölkerung, Größe, Landschaft, Klima).	☐	☐	☐
... weiß einiges über Kaliforniens Geschichte, Wirtschaft und Industrie (z.B. Obst- und Weinanbau, Tourismus, *high-tech*/Computer, Filmindustrie).	☐	☐	☐
... weiß, dass in Hermann, MO, deutsche Traditionen (z.B. Volksfeste) gepflegt werden.	☐	☐	☐

Jetzt kann ich …

	Sehr gut!	OK	Verbessern!
GRAMMATIKVERSTÄNDNIS: Ich kann …			
… Passivsätze mit *will-future* und *modals* richtig bilden und anwenden (z.B. *These strawberries will be sent to the east coast.* / *Strawberries can be grown all year round.*).	☐	☐	☐
… das *personal passive* mit Verben mit zwei Objekten (z.B. *give, offer, pay, send*) richtig verwenden (z.B. *The immigrant workers were given jobs.*).	☐	☐	☐
… Partizipien anstelle von Relativsätzen richtig verwenden (z.B. *The boy sitting at the back of the bus is Luis.* / *Illegal immigrants caught at the Mexican border are sent back.*).	☐	☐	☐
… ein Objekt + *to*-Infinitiv nach *cause, tell, want, would like* richtig verwenden (z.B. *I want you to help me.* / *He told us to find out more information.*).	☐	☐	☐
… einige Nomen, die im Englischen keine Pluralform haben, richtig verwenden (z.B. *furniture/homework/information/news is …*). Mit solchen nicht zählbaren Nomen verwende ich die Mengenangaben *some/any, a lot of/(not) much.*	☐	☐	☐
… den bestimmten Artikel richtig einsetzen. Wenn ein Nomen für einen abstrakten Begriff (z.B. *life, quality, health*) oder eine Stoffbezeichnung (z.B. *air, gold*) ganz allgemein gebraucht wird, steht es ohne *the*. *The* verwende ich bei solchen Nomen, wenn sie näher bestimmt werden (z.B. *Life is exciting for Timo.* / *The life of Missouri farmers is interesting.*).	☐	☐	☐
VOKABELVERSTÄNDNIS: Ich kann …			
… AE-Wörter für die Schule (z.B. *elementary school, middle school, schedule, grades, extracurriculars*) richtig verwenden.	☐	☐	☐
… aus Verben und Adjektiven Nomen bilden (z.B. *sad – sadness, translate – translation*).	☐	☐	☐
… Wörter, die ethnische Minderheiten und ihre Probleme beschreiben, richtig verwenden (z.B. *ethnic minority, discrimination, prejudice, illegal*).	☐	☐	☐
SKILLS – LERNEN UND ARBEITEN: Ich kann …			
… eine Gliederung (*outline*) mit Hauptpunkten und Unterthemen anfertigen, die mir beim Recherchieren und beim Ordnen meines schriftlichen Materials hilft.	☐	☐	☐

WAS ICH FÜR MEIN ENGLISCHLERNEN GETAN HABE: Ich habe …	häufig	manchmal	nie
… die Angaben im Grammar File in meinem Buch aufmerksam gelesen.	☐	☐	☐
… die Lern- und Arbeitstechniken im Skills File in meinem Buch im Unterricht und bei den Hausaufgaben gezielt eingesetzt.	☐	☐	☐
… bereits gelernte Vokabeln und Grammatik häufig aufgefrischt.	☐	☐	☐

WIE ICH MICH VERBESSERN KÖNNTE: Ich könnte …

- … im Unterricht aktiver mitarbeiten. ☐
- … ein zweisprachiges Wörterbuch häufiger verwenden. ☐
- … englische Websites zu Unterrichtsthemen gezielt recherchieren. ☐
- … mir Texte auf meiner CD häufiger anhören. ☐
- … englischsprachige Zeitschriften lesen. ☐
- … eine/n englische/n *e-friend* suchen. ☐

Unit 5 Atlanta rising

1 Atlanta ▸ *pp. 98–99*

a) *Look at the picture on p. 98 of your student's book. Do you think it's impressive? Describe what you see in a paragraph. Include these words and phrases in your description:*

freeway • grid • skyscrapers • downtown • stadium • in the foreground/background • on the right/left, etc.

I think the picture of Atlanta is ______________________

____

____

____

____

____

____

Test

b) *Have you listened to 'Atlanta's history' in your student's book? If yes, are the statements below right or wrong? Have a look at p. 99 of your student's book again. Mark a letter.*

		Right	Wrong
1	Atlanta is the capital of Alabama.	A	I
2	Atlanta was founded in 1847.	T	R
3	President Abraham Lincoln was against slavery.	C	K
4	Lincoln wanted the USA to break up into two countries.	A	L
5	In 1864 Atlanta was burned down.	N	A
6	The South won the Civil War.	E	N
7	Stith Pemberton invented a drink which is known all over the world.	B	S
8	Martin Luther King was a non-violent Civil Rights leader.	I	A
9	CNN was the world's first 24-hour news station.	L	S
10	In 1996 the Olympic Games were opened by President George Bush senior.	E	O
11	61% of Atlanta's population is black.	L	R

6201

c) *Put the letters that are marked in the correct order to make the name of the man who opened the Atlanta Olympic Games:*

____

d) *What do you remember about the events on the Atlanta timeline from 1968–2002? In your exercise book, describe three events in one or two sentences.*

In 1968 …

Fun fact

Georgia is the USA's top producer of the '3 Ps' – peanuts[1], pecans[2] and peaches[3].

[1] peanut ['pi:nʌt] *Erdnuss* [2] pecan ['pɪ:kən, AE: pɪ'kɑ:n] *Pekannuss* [3] peach [pi:tʃ] *Pfirsich*

2 WORDS All about ... the media ▸ p. 100

a) Write the answers in the crossword and find the word down.

1 Madison's favourite TV ... are crime and drama series.
2 CNN is a TV news ...
3 NPR ... good news programmes.
4 Madison doesn't listen to the ... much.
5 Madison's mom reads reports from lots of ... online.

b) Choose two of the following media. Write a paragraph each about how much/often you use them and what you use them for most. Write in your exercise book.

1 television/DVD 2 radio 3 computer/internet 4 print (books/newspapers/magazines)

The two media I use most are ... and ... I spend quite a lot of time ... I usually ...

Ideas: series • videos • soap operas • news • information • chat • surf • download • e-mails • social networking • research • music • short stories • libraries • interesting photos • fashion trends • lifestyle articles

6302

3 EVERYDAY ENGLISH MEDIATION[1] TV in the USA ▸ p. 100 • SF (p. 165) Track 9

Test

Brad, a boy from Atlanta, is staying with your neighbours, the Bergers. Brad doesn't speak much German and your neighbours don't speak much English. They ask you to mediate.

Frau B. Kannst du Brad fragen, wie er deutsches Fernsehen findet?

You *Mrs Berger wants to know what you think of German TV?*

Brad Well, my problem is that I don't understand much. But I think it's funny when I hear American actors speaking German. Yesterday I watched the Simpsons and Bart Simpson was speaking German. I don't know what he was saying, but just listening to him was real funny.

You ...

Listen to the rest of the conversation and mediate for the family and Brad. Remember, just give the most important information.

Info box

Atlanta is...

- the fastest growing city in the USA.
- one of the cleanest cities in the USA.
- maybe the 'greenest' city in the USA because of the green oak trees[2] that line[3] its streets.

Atlanta has ...

- the world's largest aquarium, opened in 2005.
- the world's busiest international airport with over 77 million passengers a year.
- 32 streets with the name 'Peachtree'.
- 41 golf courses.

[1] channel ['tʃænəl] *Fernsehsender* [2] oak tree [AE: 'oʊk tri:] *Eiche* [3] line [laɪn] *säumen*

4 EVERYDAY ENGLISH SPEAKING Talking about soap operas ▸ p. 100 Track 10

Test

Listen to the dialogue between Katie and her brother Mason. They have different opinions about TV soap operas. What do you think? Do you agree with Katie or with Mason? Make notes and prepare your arguments for or against soap operas for a three-minute talk in class. The words and phrases below will help you.

I (don't) agree with ... • In my opinion ... • My view is that ... • I think ... ,

music • actors • everyday situations • events • problems • good entertainment • modern • fantastic • awesome • cool • popular • fun • interesting • terrible • silly • boring • unrealistic

NOTES: For/Against soap operas

6404

5 TYCTWD ▸ p. 101

Test

a) *Tick (✔) the correct answer, A, B or C. You need the letters in brackets for part b).*

1 TYCTWD takes place ...

A twice a year. (A) B on the fourth Thursday in April. (W) C on the fourth Tuesday in April. (C)

2 Who participates in TYCTWD?

A All schools and all companies. (G) B All schools and some companies. (O)

C Not all companies or schools. (T)

3 What does Madison want to do on this day?

A Go to visit her dad's workplace. (Y) B Stay at home. (M) C Go to visit her mom's workplace. (E)

4 How many students usually participate in TYCTWD?

A 25 million. (N) B 2.5 million. (Y) C More than 25 million. (R)

5 Madison's mom works at ...

A the King Center. (C) B the CNN studios. (N) C Atlanta airport. (P)

6 Why didn't Madison go to her mom's workplace on TYCTWD?

A Because there was a fire there. (S) B Because they were in a traffic jam. (D)

C Because her mom decided against it. (O)

7 The idea behind the TYCTWD is ...

A to introduce kids to the world of work. (K) B to give teachers a free day. (P)

C to interest students in the company they visit. (Y)

b) *Write the letters next to your answers in the correct order to find the missing word:*

CNN is a worldwide 24-hour TV news ____________ which was founded in Atlanta.

6 READING COURSE Part 5: Text types

► p. 101 • SF (p. 164)

a) Match the description on the right to the text type on the left.

- fiction
- non-fiction

- invents stories and characters
- reports true events and facts
- uses lots of description and details
- wants to inform
- wants to entertain
- often uses direct speech
- wants the reader to think
- often gives an opinion
- often uses the passive

b) Are the following text types fiction or non-fiction? Write f or n.

- sports report n
- play ____
- technical description ____
- dictionary entry ____
- song lyrics ____
- crime report ____
- instructions ____
- short story ____
- newspaper article ____
- poem ____

c) Read the texts 1–6. You needn't understand everything. Then match the texts with a text type from b) and write fiction or non-fiction.

1 Manchester United beat Everton 3–2 in a fast and exciting match at Stamford Bridge stadium on Saturday. In the eleventh minute United's Wayne Rooney scored the first goal with a beautiful overhead shot. This was followed by a second goal just before the ...

sports report, non-fiction

2

Jack *(takes money from pocket and counts it)* Well, I'm sorry, but you needn't be so rude. Here's your money. Twenty, forty, sixty dollars. What do you need money for right now, anyway?

Will *(putting money into pocket)* That's none of your business. I just need it, OK?

Jack I thought brothers were supposed to trust each other and tell each other stuff.

Will *(getting up to leave café)* Not this time, OK?

Suzy *(enters café with expensive-looking shopping bags, sees Will)* Hi, babe! *(kisses Will on cheek)*. Oh, this must be your little brother. Cute!

Will *(quickly takes Suzy by the hand)* Come on. We're leaving.

____

3 Suspects are being questioned, but so far it is not clear whether the death of the 42-year-old Ukranian should be treated as an accident or murder. Detective Inspector G. Wood stated earlier today that police investigations ...

____

4 In case of fire:
Stay calm and act quickly. Alert others. Use the safest and nearest exit. Do not run. Do not use elevators. Close all doors as you leave the building. Inform the fire ...

____

5 It was already light. A new day was born, and this time it would be a very special, eventful day. Jessica felt as if her heart would burst with excitement in anticipation of what was to come. She had waited for this day so long. 'Come on, Jess!' cried Kitty, knocking frantically on her door. 'Everybody's waiting.'

____

6 With a gas-powered car the potential energy of the motor is converted into heat, while the electric car uses the forward momentum to recharge its batteries. The vehicle's range can be increased by up to 15%.

____

7 WRITING A story ▸ p. 101 • SF (pp. 168–169)

Test

Here's the beginning of a story about Kerstin, a 14-year old German girl who is on a visit to her aunt and uncle in Atlanta. Use your writing skills to write the middle and the end of the story. Give the story a title too. You can use the pictures for ideas or use your own imagination. Write in your exercise book. You can read out your story in class.

It was Friday night. Kerstin had been in Atlanta for just one week, so everything was strange to her. The big house in Atlanta was still strange to her too. She didn't really like being alone at night in a strange house, but she wanted to do something for the family. The baby was sleeping, everything was quiet.

Suddenly the phone rang. She jumped nervously. It stopped. Then it rang again. Should she answer it? She could only say that the family were out, but then the caller would know that anyway if she didn't answer the phone. It was still ringing. Then she thought she heard a knock at the window. Her heart started to beat loudly. Was there someone outside?

...

8 Blue box: Verbs and nouns with the same form ▸ p. 101, p. 219

a) Some verbs and nouns have the same form. Others have different forms. Complete the lists.

Verb		Noun	Verb		Noun
announce	–	*announcement*	explain	–	
attack	–	*attack*	pray	–	
cause	–		protest	–	
celebrate	–		sentence	–	
confuse	–		support	–	
drive	–		taste	–	

b) Now complete the sentences with words from a).

1 What caused the American Civil War? – Well, slavery in the southern states was not the main ________.

2 Did terrorists[1] attack Atlanta airport? – No, the fire wasn't caused by a terrorist ________________.

3 How long did it take to drive to the airport? – Well, there was a traffic jam, so it was a long ________.

4 Is the TYCTWD supported by many companies? – Oh, yes. The project enjoys a lot of ________.

c) Read through the Vocabulary section (pp. 190–221) in your student's book and look for more pairs of verbs and nouns with the same form. Write a list in your exercise book.

[1] terrorist ['terərɪst]

9 REVISION She's the girl who ... (Defining relative clauses)

▸ p. 102 • GF 10a (p. 186)

*Write sentences with **who** or **which/that**. Use the correct verb tense.*

1 Madison/girl/Atlanta/want to visit CNN with her mother

Madison is the girl from Atlanta who wanted to visit CNN with her mother.

2 Mr Young/man/work/Martin Luther King Center

3 Madison/look round/library and archives/dad/use

4 Martin Luther King/man/become/very important civil rights leader

5 'I have a dream'/speech/be called/one of the greatest speeches in US history

6709

10 Sentence comments (Relative clauses with *which* to refer to a whole clause)

▸ p. 102 • GF 10b (p. 186)

*The comments in green do not match the statements. Find the correct comment and rewrite the sentences with **which**.*

1 Madison couldn't go to the airport with her mom. That impressed her dad.

2 But maybe Madison could get a summer job with CNN. That was a big disappointment[1].

3 Madison helped her dad to put away some MLK letters. That means that lots of students visit the Center for information.

4 Madison knew the anniversary of King's death. That would be great.

5 Teachers often give their students projects on MLK. It was more interesting than she had expected.

1 *Madison couldn't go to the airport with her mom, which was a big disappointment.*

2

3

4

5

[1] disappointment [ˌdɪsəˈpɔɪntmənt] *Enttäuschung*

11 Extra People and places in my book (Non-defining relative clauses)

▸ p. 102 • GF 10c (p. 187)

a) The sentences are about people and places in your student's book. Read the extra information below, then add the correct piece of information to each sentence. Remember to use commas.

1 The Grand Canyon, ▶ *which is visited by about 5 million people every year,* is one the the world's greatest tourist attractions.

2 Caitlin, ▶ ______ visits a different national park with her family every year.

3 Las Vegas, ▶ ______ is one of the entertainment capitals of the world.

4 The main attraction in San Francisco is the Golden Gate Bridge, ▶ ______

5 English colonists, ▶ ______ founded Plymouth Colony.

6 Martin Luther King was a friend of Jesse Jackson, ▶ ______

- who was with him when he was killed
- *which is visited by about 5 million people every year*
- which is painted international orange
- which was built in the desert of Nevada
- who comes from New York
- who arrived on the Mayflower in 1621

6811

b) Add extra information. Find interesting facts in your student's book and rewrite the sentences with a relative clause.

1 The Empire State Building was opened in 1931.

The Empire State Building ______

2 The English colonists in Plymouth were helped by the Wampanoag.

The English colonists ______

12 REVISION Some history (The definite article)

▸ p. 102 • GF 8 (p. 185)

Complete the sentences with **the** *where necessary.*

1 Before the Civil War ______ life was very good for rich white plantation owners[1] in the south.

But ______ life of their slaves was very hard.

2 ______ history has often shown that people see violence and war as the answer to a country's problems.

That's why ______ history of the Civil Rights Movement in America is especially[2] interesting.

3 In 1963 there were many black protests in Birmingham, Alabama. King's supporters did not want ______ violence, but ______ violence of the Birmingham police shocked the nation.

4 Martin Luther King hated ______ war, but many African Americans had to fight in ______ war against Vietnam.

5 ______ quality of ______ life for African Americans has improved, but there are still three times more poor black people than poor white people in the USA.

[1] owner ['əʊnə(r)] *Besitzer/in* [2] especially [ɪ'speʃəli] *besonders*

13 LISTENING Malcolm X ▸ p. 103 Track 11

Test

a) Listen to the information about Malcolm X. Then complete the text.

Malcolm X was born in Nebraska in the year _____. His real name was Malcolm _____. Like Martin Luther King he first became a _____, then a black speaker and civil rights leader. But he _____ with King that non-violent protest was the only way to fight for equal rights. Black people wanted _____, and many thought that it was coming too slowly. Malcolm X believed that blacks should fight for equal _____ not with words, but with violent _____. He said that white racists[1] only spoke the language of _____, not the language of peace[2].

Many young blacks followed Malcolm X. There were riots in the big cities of America and many people were killed. Malcolm X was shot in 1965, while he was giving a _____ in New York.

b) What was the main difference between the two civil rights leaders Martin Luther King and Malcolm X? Listen to your CD again. In your exercise book, write a paragraph in your own words.

Now you

Choose one statement. Do you agree or disagree with it? Write your ideas in your exercise book (about 120 words).

1 Problems cannot be solved[3] by the use of violence.
2 If you want change, you have to do something.
3 Martin Luther King's dream has come true.

I agree/disagree with statement 1, that problems cannot be solved by the use of violence. In my opinion, ...

14 German 'während' ▸ p. 103

*Complete the sentences with **during** or **while**.*

1 Before the American Civil War white plantation owners got rich while their black slaves had a terrible life.

2 _____ the Civil War Atlanta was burned down.

3 Over 620,000 Americans were killed _____ the years 1861 to 1865.

4 In 1884, _____ Pemberton was trying to help people feel better, he invented a world-famous drink.

5 Martin Luther King led the non-violent Civil Rights Movement, _____ others wanted to fight violence with violence.

6914

6 _____ the years 1955 to his death in 1968 King worked very hard for the rights of African Americans.

[1] racist ['reɪsɪst] *Rassist/in* [2] peace [piːs] *Frieden* [3] solve [sɒlv] *lösen*

15 STUDY SKILLS Research ▸ p. 103 • SF (p. 158)

*a) What is important when you do research? Write **Y** (Yes) or **N** (No) next to the statements.*

- use only Wikipedia ___N___
- use only one good source ______
- use more than one source ______
- try to use at least one English source ______
- take notes in your own words ______
- always take notes in your own language ______
- always use full sentences for your notes ______
- look for answers to the 5 Ws (Who, What, When, Where, Why + How) ______
- copy whole sentences from your sources ______
- use only key words for internet research ______

b) Now use the internet and/or other sources to find information about Rosa Parks, another important African American in the US Civil Rights Movement. Use the information in a) for your research. Make notes, then write a short text with the most important information in your exercise book. Find answers to the following questions:

- What happened on 1st December, 1955?
- Who was James Blake?
- What was the Montgomery Bus Boycott, and why was it important?

16 WORDS Word building (Prefixes and suffixes) ▸ p. 103

a) Add a prefix or a suffix from the box to make a new word. Use some more than once.

-able • -al • dis- • -er • -ful • il- • im- • in- • -less • non- • -or • un-

1 _dis_ agree	5 edit ______	9 forget ______	13 success ______
2 depend ______	6 ______ possible	10 ______ -violent	14 ______ legal
3 invent ______	7 home ______	11 ______ healthy	15 environment ______
4 sleep ______	8 ______ advantage	12 ______ credible	16 paint ______

b) Choose five words from a), two with a prefix and three with a suffix. Write a sentence with each.

1 _My friend thinks growing up in two cultures makes life difficult, but I disagree._

2 ______________________

3 ______________________

4 ______________________

5 ______________________

7016 6 ______________________

17 Extra Background File THE SOUTH ▸ pp. 104–105

Test

a) What have you learned about the American South? Tick (✔) the correct answer, A, B or C. If you are not sure, look at pp. 104–105 of your student's book again. You need the letters in brackets in part b).

1 How many states make up the American South?

A Eight. (D) B Nine. (N) C Eleven. (E)

2 Which of the following states does not belong to the American South?

A North Carolina. (U) B North Dakota. (A) C Georgia. (E)

3 Which state was named after a British queen?

A South Carolina. (S) B Virginia. (A) C Louisiana. (H)

4 Which state was the home of the 42nd US president, Bill Clinton?

A Alabama. (P) B Tennessee. (H) C Arkansas. (N)

5 This state played an important role in the African-American fight for civil rights. The Montgomery Bus Boycott took place here.

A Alabama. (R) B Mississippi. (V) C Georgia. (B)

6 This state is named after the largest river in North America.

A Missouri. (R) B Georgia. (I) C Mississippi. (D)

7 This state is the home of many world-famous companies, including CNN.

A Georgia. (L) B Arkansas. (N) C Louisiana. (I)

8 This state is famous for its country music. It's also the home of a famous national park.

A Alabama. (L) B South Carolina. (E) C Tennessee. (C)

9 The US presidents George Washington and Thomas Jefferson came from this state.

A North Carolina. (E) B Virginia. (G) C Arkansas. (M)

b) Now write the letters in brackets next to your answers in the boxes below. If your answers are correct, the letters make the name of the home of 'the king of rock and roll'.

9	5	3	8	1	7	2	4	6

c) Which of the Southern states would you like to visit? What would you like to see there, and why? Write a paragraph in your exercise book.

If I had the chance, I think I would like to visit …

Georgia

Louisiana

18 WORKING WITH THE TEXT Melba's story ▸ pp. 111–114

a) Read pp. 111–114 of your student's book again. Which of these headlines is true for the events in Little Rock? Tick (✔) A, B or C.

A Little Rock Nine welcomed at Central High School

B LITTLE ROCK NINE ENTER HIGH SCHOOL WITH HELP OF US SOLDIERS

C President bans black students from Little Rock Central High

b) Say in one sentence what these people did.

1 The ticket man at the merry-go-round didn't let Melba ride on the ______

______

2 The Supreme Court ______

3 The white people in Little Rock ______

______

4 The Governor of Arkansas ______

______

5 The US President ______

6 The soldiers ______

7 Danny ______

______

8 The McCabe family ______

______

c) Go through the text again and write notes about the brave things Melba did.

NOTES

______

______

______

______

______

d) Do you think Melba was a hero? Use your notes from c) and write a short essay (about 120 words) in your exercise book.

1 Write the missing words.

1 Madison's mom works for the TV news ________________ CNN.

2 Madison's favourite programmes are weekly crime and ________________ series.

3 When Madison knew the date of Martin Luther King's death, her dad was ________________ .

4 The Civil Rights Movement wanted ________________ rights for black and white Americans.

5 Shirley Franklin was elected first black woman ________________ of Atlanta in 2002.

7301 *6* Not all US companies or schools ________________ in Take Your Child to Work Day.

2 Use who, which and that once each.

1 Should people break laws __________ are bad?

7302 *2* Martin Luther King, __________ had worked hard for equal rights for 12 years, was murdered in 1968.

3 Mom was called to report on a big fire at the airport, __________ I found pretty exciting.

3 Nouns from verbs

Write six nouns which have the same form as six verbs in the box. Write their German meanings too.

1 ________________ *4* ________________

2 ________________ *5* ________________

7303 *3* ________________ *6* ________________

apply • delay • elect • explain
hug • interrupt • prevent
protest • scream • smoke
solve • support

4 STUDY SKILLS Research

Find and tick (✔) the five correct statements.

When you do research, you should ...

- always use more than one source. ______
- copy whole sentences. ______
- make notes in your own words. ______
- try to use English sources too. ______
- never name your sources. ______
- think of the 5 Ws to find useful facts. ______
- 7304 name the source(s) of your information. ______

20 points

Now you

7305 7306 *Comment on this statement: 'Nothing has changed in America since the 1960s'. Brainstorm your ideas, then say why you agree or disagree. Think of key words which you can use on the internet. Write about 120 words in your exercise book.*

1 WORDS Lists ▸ after Unit 1

Find and write the group words at the top of the lists. Then write the words in the correct lists.

transport • championship • tube • sport • people • ambulance • editor • holidays • sights • paramedic • ferry • abroad • tram • tent • plane • running track • neighbour • goal • stadium • husband • accommodation • athletics • beach • adult

1 Transport	2 S ______	3 P ______	4 H ______
tube			

7401

2 Questions (Simple present) ▸ after Unit 1

Make questions with question words. Use the words in brackets and the simple present.

1 Caitlin lives in New York. (Madison?) Where does Madison live?

2 Madison comes from Atlanta. (Jake?) ______

3 Caitlin likes cycling and hiking. (Gracie and Luis?) ______

4 Luis speaks two languages. (Jake?) ______

7402 5 Jakes starts school at 8.20. (Luis and Caitlin?) ______

3 The taxi is waiting (Simple present or present progressive) ▸ after Unit 1

Complete with the correct form of the verb in brackets: simple present or present progressive.

Mum Come on! Hurry! The taxi is waiting (wait). We have to (have to) leave for the airport now.

Sam I ______ (still, pack) my bag. The plane ______ (not leave) until lunchtime. Why ______ (Mum, always, get) nervous every time we ______ (go) on holiday?

Ann Well, something usually ______ (go) wrong. Somebody ______ (always, forget) something.

Sam Oh. But Dad ______ (not get) nervous, does he? What ______ (he, do) just now?

Ann He ______ (already, sit) in the taxi, I ______ (think).

7403 *Dad* Well, no, I ______ (not sit) in the taxi. Erm … I ______ (look) for my passport[1] …

[1] passport ['pɑːspɔːt] *Reisepass*

4 We went up the Stratosphere Tower (Simple past) ▸ after Unit 1

Complete the dialogue with simple past forms of the verbs in brackets.

Kate Tom! You're back! How was (be) your trip to Las Vegas? Did you have (you, have) a good time?

Tom Oh, yes, thanks. I ________ (have) a great time.

Kate So, where ________ (you, go) and what ________ (you, see)?

Tom Well, I ________ (do) a tour of all the theme hotels with my cousin Eli, and my aunt and uncle ________ (plan) a day tour to Death Valley. The scenery was awesome. The views ________ (be) fantastic.

Kate And what ________ (you, do) in the evenings?

Tom One evening we ________ (go) up the Stratosphere Tower. I ________ (not enjoy) going up in the fast lift much. I just ________ (close) my eyes and ________ (try) to think of something else. But I ________ (take) some cool photos from the top. We ________ (not go) to any shows – too expensive. And no, before you ask, I ________ (not meet) my dream girl ...

5 It was raining ... (Simple past or past progressive) ▸ after Unit 1

Underline the correct verb form in the brackets.

1 When we (were arriving/arrived) in New York, it (rained/was raining).
2 The sun suddenly (came/was coming) out when we (were taking/took) photos of the Statue of Liberty.
3 We (saw/were seeing) lots of interesting people when we (were walking/walked) through Central Park.
4 Just as I (was crossing/crossed) Times Square, a man (was asking/asked) me something in German.
7505 5 As I (was shopping/shopped) in Macy's, I suddenly (realized/was realizing) that I had forgotten my money.

6 Washington (Present perfect with since/for)

Complete with ***since*** *or* ***for****.*

1 The USA has had 50 states ________ over 50 years.
2 Washington has been the capital of the USA ________ 1800.
3 US presidents have lived in the White House ________ more than 200 years.
4 President Obama has lived in the White House ________ January, 2009.
5 ________ it was completed in 1928, the Capitol building has survived three earthquakes.
7506 6 We should go to Washington again soon. We haven't been there ________ almost a year.

7 They've all been there (Simple past or present perfect) ▸ after Unit 1

Fill in simple past or present perfect forms.

Lucy, Brad and Kelly *have all been* (all, be) to the Grand Canyon. They *went* (go) there in the last summer vacation. Here's what they ________ (say) after their trip.

Kelly The Grand Canyon is the most exciting place I ________ (ever, visit). And the walk on the glass floor is the scariest thing I ________ (ever, do) in my life.

Lucy We ________ (stay) at the Canyon for three days. I ________ (never, see) anything so beautiful. It ________ (be) so awesome!

Brad If you ________ (not be) to the Grand Canyon, you really must go. It's fantastic. It ________ (take) us three days to get there, but we ________ (enjoy) every minute of the trip. I ________ (see) some nice places in the US, but nothing like the Grand Canyon.

7607

8 WORDS Word families (Nouns from verbs) ▸ after Unit 1

Write a noun from each verb. Sometimes the noun is the same as the verb. If you know two nouns, write both.

	Verb		Noun		Verb		Noun
1	announce	–	*announcement*	*7*	explain	–	________
2	argue	–	________	*8*	fly	–	________
3	arrive	–	________	*9*	hope	–	________
4	collect	–	________	*10*	invite	–	________
5	cook	–	________	*11*	live	–	________
6	describe	–	________	*12*	murder	–	________

9 Ride carefully! (Adjective or adverb) ▸ after Unit 1

Complete with the adjective or adverb form of the word in brackets.

1 My dad is a taxi-driver in New York, so he knows the city traffic ________ (good).

2 He always tells me to ride ________ (careful) when I'm on my bike.

3 He says most people drive ________ (safe), but there are always some ________ (bad) drivers who go too ________ (fast).

4 My dad says 'Sometimes you have to be ________ (careful) on the sidewalks too. Some kids skate ________ (dangerous), so you're not ________ (safe) anywhere in a big city.'

7609

10 Florida facts (Passive) ▸ after Unit 1 • GF 4a–b (p. 179)

Complete with the passive: simple present or simple past.

1 Florida _is_ often _called_ (call) 'the Sunshine State'. Because of its beautiful beaches it ________ (visit) by millions of tourists every year.

2 Florida ________ (discover) by the Spanish in 1513.

3 Oranges ________ (grow) in Florida. They ________ (sell) all over the world.

4 Spanish ________ (speak) by more than two million people.

5 The theme park Walt Disney World ________ (open) in Orlando in 1971.

6 The world's largest Hard Rock Café ________ (build) in Orlando too.

7 Florida ________ (hit) by hurricanes almost every year. In 2007, 21 people ________ (kill).

7710 Hundreds of buildings ________ (destroy) and homes ________ (lose).

11 If I have enough money... (Conditional sentences 1 and 2) ▸ after Unit 1 • GF 2a–b (p. 175)

Complete the sentences with the correct forms of the verbs.

1 A: If I _have_ (have) enough money in summer, maybe I _'ll go_ (go) to the USA with a friend.

2 B: Great! Where ________ (you, stay) if you go?

3 A: Well, maybe California, for three weeks. We'd take our camping gear if we ________ (stay) at places along the coast.

4 B: Cool. You ________ (be able to) swim in the Pacific every day if you were close to a beach.

If I ever ________ (visit) California, I'd want to see the theme parks, Disneyland or Sea World.

7711 5 A: That would be cool too. But if we went to theme parks, we ________ (spend) all our money in the first week!

12 Jeff's presentation (have to, be allowed to, be able to) ▸ after Unit 1

Complete with the correct form of the modal in brackets. Be careful with the tense!

I _have to_ (have to) give a presentation about George Washington, but my computer is broken. Dad is in London and I ________ (be allowed to) use his computer when he isn't at home. Yesterday I ________ (have to) go to the library. I ________ (be able to) get some information, but not enough. I ________ (have to) ask my friend for help tomorrow. I hope he ________ (be able to) download some stuff for me. If I don't finish my presentation, I ________ (not be allowed) go out on Saturday.

13 The Grand Canyon (Contact clauses) ▸ after Unit 1

a) Find sentences where you don't need **who** *or* **that** *and write them again as contact clauses. You need the letters in brackets in b).*

US park rangers protect the animals that live in national parks (I) and the tourists who visit the park every year (N). There's lots of information that the rangers can give you (T). For example, they can tell you about the Native Americans who first lived in the Canyon area (N). In national parks there are things that tourists must or mustn't do (U). There are rules that you must follow if you want to be safe (A). One rule says you mustn't make fires in places that might be dangerous (D). There are also trails that tourists mustn't take if they aren't fit (H).

1 *There's lots of information the rangers can give you.* ____ *T*

2 ____________________ ____

3 ____________________ ____

7813 4 ____________________ ____

b) Now write down the letters in brackets after the four sentences. Order the letters to find the name of a state close to Arizona.

The state is ▸ ____________ .

14 A postcard from the USA (Indirect speech) ▸ after Unit 1 • *GF 3a (p. 177)*

Your cousin Matt is on holiday in the USA. You get a postcard from him. Tell a friend what he wrote.

Hi!

We're driving down the east coast from New York to Florida. So far we've driven through four states. We saw the White House – but I didn't visit the president because he wasn't at home. There are lots of interesting places to see, but the trip gets a bit boring sometimes. It will take two more days to get to Miami. Then I'm going to surf and play beach volleyball all day!

1 My cousin Matt wrote that *they were driving down the east coast from New York to Florida.*

2 He wrote that ____________________

3 He said that ____________________

4 But he explained that ____________________

____

5 He said that ____________________

____

6 He wrote that ____________________

7814 7 He wrote that in Miami ____________________

- Hier kannst du deine Antworten im Checkpoint überprüfen. Falls du Probleme mit den jeweiligen Aufgaben hattest, folge den Lernhilfen in der rechten Spalte. Die Verweise beziehen sich auf dein Schülerbuch oder dein Workbook.
- Deine Punktzahl kannst du ermitteln, indem du dir für jede richtige Lösung einen Punkt gibst. Schreib deine Gesamtpunktzahl in das gelbe Kästchen unten links.

1 What are these places?

1 deli
2 downtown
3 skyscraper(s)
4 block
5 gas station

5 P.

- Lies dir im Skills File in deinem Buch den Abschnitt zu *Learning words* durch (S. 155).
- Lern die Wörter mithilfe des Vocabulary (Buch: S. 194–197).

2 Write the missing words.

1 vacation
2 line
3 schedule
4 sidewalk
5 first floor
6 grade

6 P.

- Lern die AE-Wörter mithilfe der blauen Kästen auf den S. 194 und 198 in deinem Buch.

3 Complete the sentences.

1 planning
2 meeting
3 finding
4 taking
5 travelling

5 P.

- Schau dir Grammar File 1 zum Gerundium in deinem Buch (S. 173–174) oder hinten im Skills File *kompakt* in deinem Workbook noch einmal an.
- Löse die Aufgaben 6 (S. 24) und 8a (S. 25) im Practice-Teil in deinem Buch.

4 Working out the meaning of words

1 Vorfahren
2 Verfolgung
3 Arbeitslosigkeit
4 Schiffsladung

4 P.

- Im Skills File (S. 163) in deinem Buch oder im Skills File *kompakt* hinten in deinem Workbook kannst du dir die wichtigsten Punkte zu *Working out the meaning of words* durchlesen.

Now you (Ideas)

Good things: a rich, multi-cultural city with world-famous sights / important tourist and international business centre / interesting history (Ellis Island, Liberty, etc.) / Broadway theatres, concerts, opera, famous museums, art galleries/ Central Park / international airports, subway / a city that never sleeps is exciting

Bad things: traffic day and night / noise / crowded city streets / can take a long time to get around / poor areas (e.g. the Bronx) / expensive city to live in / high prices for houses and apartments

Ich habe ______ Punkte von 20.

20–18	Sehr gut. Weiter so!
17–15	Schon recht gut.
Unter 15	Genauer lernen!

- Um Ideen über New York zu sammeln, kannst du dir die Unit 1 in deinem Buch noch einmal anschauen oder im Internet recherchieren.
- Lies dir im Skills File den Abschnitt zu *Brainstorming* durch (Buch: S. 166), um deine Ideen besser ordnen zu können.
- Um den Gebrauch des *simple present* sicherer zu beherrschen, kannst du im Revision-Block (S. 74) in deinem Workbook die Übungen 2 und 3 machen.
- Trage deinen kurzen Vortrag über New York laut vor.

1 Write the missing words.

5 P.

1 *abbreviation*
2 *because of*
3 *secret*
4 *staff*
5 *interrupt*

2 Complete with the correct verb forms.

2 P.

1 *hadn't been*
2 *wouldn't have found out*

3 Report Gracie's questions.

3 P.

1 *had been*
2 *had hunted*
3 *were allowed*

4 What did they tell Gracie?

2 P.

1 *to ask*
2 *not to forget*

5 Complete the text.

6 P.

... a *handout* ... *before* the ... *follow* it better ... your *name* and the *date* ... give *sources* ...

Now you (Ideas)

Dear ..., We did something really interesting yesterday. Our history teacher took us on a day trip to the ... / Museum in ... / First we ... / After that ... / Then ... / Before we... / We saw lots of old ... / I liked the ... best / It was very interesting and I learned some cool facts because I asked lots of questions and read all the information / We have to write a report about the visit, so I must stop now and start my homework. Write soon, Love ...

Ich habe ______ Punkte von 18.

18–16 Sehr gut. Weiter so!
15–13 Schon recht gut.
Unter 13 Genauer lernen!

Falls du Probleme hattest:

- Schau dir im Skills File in deinem Buch den Abschnitt zu *Learning words* an (S. 155).
- Lern die Wörter (Buch: S. 201–204).

- Im Grammar File 2c (Buch: S. 176, Workbook: S. 85) erfährst du, wie du *conditional sentences 3* bilden kannst. Üben kannst du diese Bedingungssätze im Practice-Teil mithilfe der Übungen 6 und 7a (Buch: S. 47).
- Wenn du die *conditional sentences 1* und *2* wiederholen möchtest, kannst du im Revision-Block die Aufgabe 11 (Workbook: S. 77) lösen. Im Grammar File 2a–b findest du Informationen zu diesen Bedingungssätzen (Buch: S. 175, Workbook: S. 85).

- Schau dir Grammar File 3b zu Fragen in der indirekten Rede noch einmal an (Buch: S. 177–178, Workbook: S. 86).
- Löse die Aufgabe 11a im Practice-Teil (Buch: S. 49).
- Im Revision-Block kannst du die indirekte Rede mit der Übung 14 (Workbook: S. 78) wiederholen. Grammar File 3a gibt dir allgemeine Informationen zur indirekten Rede (Buch: S. 177, Workbook: S. 86).

- Lies dir zu Aufforderungen und Bitten in der indirekten Rede Grammar File 3c durch (Buch: S. 178, Workbook: S. 86).
- Mach die Übung 12a im Practice-Teil noch einmal (Buch: S. 49).

- Im Skills File (Buch: S. 160) kannst du dir die wichtigsten Punkte für eine *presentation* und ein *handout* anschauen.
- Lies dir auch den blauen Kasten zu *handouts* in deinem Buch durch (S. 42).

- Wie du deine Ideen ordnen und deine E-Mail strukturieren kannst, kannst du im Skills File unter dem Punkt *Writing course* nachlesen (Buch: S. 168–169, Workbook: S. 84).
- Um das *simple past* zu wiederholen, löse im Revision-Block die Aufgaben 4, 5 und 7 (Workbook: S. 75, 76).

1 Write the missing words.

6 P.

1 bilingual
2 illegal
3 attitude
4 prejudiced
5 education
6 advantage

Falls du Probleme hattest:

- Lies dir im Skills File den Abschnitt zu *Learning words* durch (Buch: S. 155).
- Lern die Wörter mithilfe des Vocabulary (Buch: S. 207–212).

2 Complete the word families.

6 P.

1 wealthy
2 thought
3 environmental
4 succeed
5 discrimination
6 warning

- Schau dir die Wörter noch einmal im Vocabulary an und lern sie (Buch: S. 207–212).
- Im Revision-Block gibt es auch eine Übung zu *word families* (Workbook: S. 76, Übung 8).

3 What does she want them to do?

2 P.

1 Mrs Morales wants Luis to do the shopping.
2 She'd like Maria to lay the table for supper

- Im Grammar File 6a erfährst du, wie du den *to*-Infinitiv in Verbindung mit bestimmten Verben und einem Objekt richtig gebrauchst (Buch: S. 182, Workbook: S. 87).
- Übe diese Struktur mithilfe der Aufgabe 15 im Practice-Teil (Buch: S. 70).

4 Write the sentences in the personal passive.

2 P.

1 Luis was shown round the movie studios.
2 The people on the tour were given lots of information.

- Schau dir Grammar File 4 zum Passiv noch einmal an (Buch: S. 179–180, Workbook: S. 86–87).
- Wiederhole die Aufgaben 6–8 und 10a im Practice-Teil (Buch: S. 66–67).
- Im Revision-Block findest du die Übung 10 zum Passiv (Workbook: S. 77).

5 Describe the twins Gina and Fay.

2 P.

1 The twin sitting on the horse/feeding the horse is Gina.
2 And the twin feeding the horse/sitting on the horse is Fay – I think.

- Um Partizipien sicherer zu gebrauchen, solltest du dir Grammar File 5 anschauen (Buch: S. 181, Workbook: S. 87).
- Löse die Aufgabe 12a im Practice-Teil noch einmal (Buch: S. 69).

Now you (Ideas)

For many people California is a dreamland / sunny weather all year / rich state because of its many industries: agriculture (wine, fruit and vegetables) / Silicon Valley (computer and software industry) / movie industry / theme parks / lots of activities for tourists: beaches / beautiful coast / surfing / national parks / theme parks / cities like San Francisco and L.A. / but the state also has some problems: earthquakes / forest fires / pollution of beaches and ocean / crime and air pollution in big cities

- Suche in der Unit 3 in deinem Buch nach Informationen über die relevanten Punkte über Kalifornien. Du kannst auch im Internet recherchieren.
- Die *writing skills* kannst du dir im Skills File noch einmal anschauen (Buch: S. 168–169, Workbook: S. 84).

Ich habe ______ Punkte von 18.

18–16	Sehr gut. Weiter so!
15–13	Schon recht gut.
Unter 13	Genauer lernen!

Falls du Probleme hattest:

1 Write the missing words.

1 *Winemaking* 4 *apply for*
2 *ancestors* 5 *Government*
3 *extracurricular* 6 *elementary*

6 P.

- Lies dir im Skills File den Abschnitt zu *Learning words* durch (Buch: S. 155).
- Lern die Wörter (Buch: S. 213–217).

2 Underline the correct word or phrase.

1 (a little/a few) (a lot of/many) (a few/a little)
2 (less/a few) (fewer/the least)

5 P.

- Über die Besonderheiten von nicht zählbaren Nomen erfährst du etwas im Grammar File 7 (Buch: S. 183–184, Workbook: S. 88).
- Wiederhole die Übungen 5a–b und 6 im Practice-Teil (Buch: S. 86).

3 Add the where you need it.

1 Jake: *the*
Timo: *–*
2 *–* *The*

4 P.

- Wie du den bestimmten Artikel *the* gebrauchst, erfährst du im Grammar File 8 (Buch: S. 185, Workbook: S. 88).
- Löse die Aufgabe 9 im Practice-Teil (Buch: S. 88).

4 Find and tick (✓) the five correct statements.

- give only the most important information from the original text. ✓
- tell the reader what the text or story is about in the first few sentences. ✓
- explain **who** does **what**, **where**, **when** and **why**. ✓
- give lots of details. ___
- use the simple present and your own words. ✓
- leave out examples and direct speech. ✓
- use lots of adjectives for description and comparisons. ___

5 P.

- Im Skills File kannst du noch einmal nachlesen, was beim *summary writing* wichtig ist (Buch: S. 167).
- Schau dir auch den blauen Kasten auf S. 89 in deinem Buch an.

Now you (Ideas)

There are a few important differences between US and German schools: US school types (elementary, middle/ junior high, high school) / school day (afternoon school, hot lunch in school) / US grade system (A–F) / longer summer vacation / importance of extracurricular activities and sports / cheerleaders for school teams

- Informationen über amerikanische Schulen findest du in der Unit 4 in deinem Buch und in den Aufgaben 2–4 in deinem Workbook (S. 47–48).
- Ordne deine Gedanken und strukturiere deinen Text in sinnvolle Absätze (*Writing course*: Buch S. 168–169, Workbook S. 84).

Ich habe ______ Punkte von 20.

20–18	Sehr gut. Weiter so!
17–15	Schon recht gut.
Unter 15	Genauer lernen!

Falls du Probleme hattest:

1 Write the missing words.

6 P.

1 network
2 drama
3 impressed
4 equal
5 mayor
6 participate

- Lern die Wörter (Buch: S. 217–221).

2 Use who, which and that once each.

3 P.

1 that
2 who
2 which

- Grammar File 10 gibt dir Informationen über die Relativsätze und die Relativpronomen (Buch: S. 186, Workbook: S. 88).
- Wiederhole die Übungen 7 und 8 im Practice-Teil (Buch: S. 109).
- Im Revision-Block findest du auch eine Übung zu Relativsätzen (Workbook: S. 78, Übung 13).

3 Nouns from verbs

6 P.

1 delay, Verspätung
2 hug, Umarmung
3 protest, Protest
4 scream, Schrei
5 smoke, Rauch
6 support, Unterstützung

- Schau dir den blauen Kasten im Vocabulary an (Buch: S. 219).
- Löse die Aufgabe 6a–b im Practice-Teil (Buch: S. 108).

4 STUDY SKILLS Research

5 P.

- always use more than one source. ✓
- copy whole sentences.
- make notes in your own words. ✓
- try to use English sources too. ✓
- never name your sources.
- think of the 5 Ws to find useful facts. ✓
- name the source(s) of your information. ✓

- Im Skills File erfährst du, wie du beim Recherchieren am besten vorgehen solltest (Buch: S. 158).
- Lies dir auch den blauen Kasten zu *research* auf S. 103 in deinem Buch durch.

Now you (Ideas)

I agree/don't agree with the statement that ... / I think that the situation of African Americans has improved a lot since the Civil Rights Movement / more blacks complete high school / more blacks study and get good jobs / blacks world-famous in some sports (e.g. boxing, basketball, American football) / in music / film / politics / President Obama / situation of blacks much better but still not equal to whites / more blacks than whites without education, without jobs / still prejudice and discrimination against blacks

- Wenn dir die Informationen über das Thema in der Unit 5 nicht ausreichen, kannst du im Internet mehr recherchieren.
- Achte darauf, dass du deine Meinung mit Argumenten stützt.
- Strukturiere deinen Text (*Writing course*: Buch S. 168–169, Workbook S. 84).

Ich habe ______ Punkte von 20.

20–18	Sehr gut. Weiter so!
17–15	Schon recht gut.
Unter 15	Genauer lernen!

LISTENING SKILLS ▶ *SF p. 161*

Listening for gist:
Konzentriere dich beim ersten Hören auf allgemeine Informationen, z. B. die Personen (unterschiedliche Stimmen), das Thema, die Umgebung (Geräusche), die Atmosphäre (die Sprechweise der Leute).

Listening for detail:
- Mach dir noch einmal bewusst, worauf du genau achten willst (Hörauftrag), besonders bei Durchsagen (*announcements*), die du vielleicht nur einmal hören kannst.
- Lass dich nicht von Einzelheiten oder Geräuschen ablenken.
- Manche Signalwörter machen es dir leichter, den Hörtext zu verstehen.
  Aufzählung: **and**, **another**, **too**; Gegensatz: **although**, **but**
  Grund, Folge: **because**, **so**, **so that**; Vergleich: **larger/older/... than**, **as ... as**, **more**, **most**; Reihenfolge: **before**, **after**, **then**, **next**, **later**, **when**, **at last**, **at the same time**
- Auch andere Details wie z. B. die Stimme, der Akzent oder der Tonfall des Sprechers oder der Sprecherin können dir helfen, Informationen über seine oder ihre Gefühle, Herkunft usw. zu bekommen.

READING COURSE ▶ *SF pp. 163–164*

Working out the meaning of words
1. Bilder und Zeichen erklären und ergänzen oft Dinge aus dem Text. Schau sie dir deshalb vor und nach dem Lesen genau an.
2. Manche Wörter erklären sich aus dem Textzusammenhang, z. B. *When we **reached** the station, Judy bought our tickets.*
3. Zu manchen englischen Wörtern fallen dir vielleicht deutsche, französische oder lateinische Wörter ein, die ähnlich geschrieben oder ausgesprochen werden, z. B. **excellent**, **millionaire**, **nation**, **reality**.
4. Es gibt neue Wörter, in denen du bekannte Teile entdecken kannst, z. B. **friendliness**, **helpless**, **understandable**, **gardener**, **tea bag**, **waiting room**.

Skimming and Scanning
Beim **Skimming** überfliegst du einen Text schnell, um dir einen **Überblick** zu verschaffen. Du willst dabei herausfinden, worum es in dem Text geht. Achte dabei auf
- die **Überschrift**,
- die **Zwischenüberschriften** und hervorgehobene Wörter oder Sätze,
- die **Bilder** und **Bildunterschriften**,
- den **ersten Satz** und den **letzten Satz** jedes Absatzes,
- **Grafiken**, **Statistiken** und die **Quelle** des Textes.

Beim **Scanning** suchst du nach **bestimmten Informationen**. Dazu suchst du den Text nach Schlüsselwörtern *(key words)* ab und liest nur dort genauer, wo du sie findest.

Finding the main ideas of a text
1. Jeder Text hat ein Thema mit mindestens einer Hauptaussage, z. B.: *Drinking soda is one of the worst things you can do to your health.*
   Diese Hauptaussage findest du oft im **ersten Absatz**.
2. Die Hauptaussage wird in der Regel durch weitere Aussagen bzw. Gedanken unterstützt, z. B.: *Experts agree that sugary soft drinks and fast food are the main reasons why so many American teenagers are fat.*
3. Diese weiteren Aussagen bzw. Gedanken werden oft durch Beispiele und Begründungen ergänzt, z. B.: *About 7% of the calories that they take in come from soft drinks alone.*

Careful reading
Schwierige Texte musst du besonders sorgfältig und konzentriert lesen, damit du alle darin enthaltenen Informationen und Gedanken verstehst.

1. Lies den Text genau. Welches sind seine wesentlichen Aussagen?
2. Manchmal findest du die Antwort auf eine Frage nicht deutlich formuliert an einer Stelle im Text, sondern du musst dir diese Antwort aus einzelnen Informationen erschließen, die du an verschiedenen Stellen im Text findest.

Text types: fiction and non-fiction
Fiktionale Texte sind z. B. Kurzgeschichten und Romane. Der Autor wählt Figuren (*characters*) aus und erzählt von ihren Gefühlen und Handlungen, von deren Motiven und Hintergründen. Die Handlungen finden in einem oder mehreren Handlungsrahmen statt, z. B. an einem Ort, zu einer bestimmten Zeit und unter bestimmten Umständen (*setting*). Die Ereignisse können aus verschiedenen Perspektiven erzählt werden (*point of view*). Oft verwendet der Autor für seine Geschichte eine anschauliche Sprache, z. B. ausschmückende Adjektive, Metaphern, Vergleiche, direkte Rede oder er lässt den Leser an den Gedanken seiner Figuren oder des Erzählers teilhaben.
Nicht-fiktionale Texte sind z. B. Berichte in Zeitungen, wissenschaftliche Artikel, Aufsätze oder Kommentare. Hier informiert der Autor über ein Thema der realen Welt oder nimmt Stellung dazu.
Es gibt auch Texte, die ein **Mischform** aus beiden Textarten sind.

MEDIATION SKILLS ▶ *SF p. 165*

Manchmal musst du zwischen zwei Sprachen vermitteln. Das nennt man **mediation**.
- Übersetze nicht alles wörtlich, sondern gib den Sinn wieder.
- Gib nur das Wesentliche weiter, lass Unwichtiges weg.
- Verwende kurze und einfache Sätze.
- Wenn du ein Wort nicht kennst, umschreibe es oder ersetze es durch ein anderes Wort.

REVISION Writing course ▶ *SF pp. 168–169*

The steps of writing

1. Brainstorming – Ideen sammeln und ordnen
2. Schreiben. Dabei achte darauf,
- deine Sätze zu verbinden und auszubauen *(Writing better sentences:* **at 7 o'clock**, **later**, **suddenly**, **then**, **and**, **because**, **although**, **nervous**, **beautiful**...*)*,
- deinen Text gut zu strukturieren *(Using paragraphs: beginning, middle, end, topic sentence:* **My trip to ... was fantastic**/... **is famous for** ... *interessante Einstiegssätze:* **Gues what happened to me today!***)*,
- bei einem Bericht die 5 Ws abzudecken *(Writing a report:* **Who? What? Where? Why?** *und* **How?***)*,
- bei einem Leserbrief an eine Zeitschrift eine höfliche Anrede und Schlussformel zu verwenden *(Writing a letter to a magazine:* **Dear**..., **I agree/disagree with**..., **I think**..., **That is why**..., **For example**, ... **Yours sincerely**, **yours***)*.
3. Deinen Text inhaltlich und sprachlich überprüfen *(Correcting your text)*

Unit 1

GF 1 The gerund

▸ *GF pp. 173–175*

a) Use and form

Flying is exciting. **Fliegen** ist aufregend.
Travelling makes me tired.
Reisen macht mich müde.
Taking **a taxi** is quite expensive.
Mit dem Taxi zu fahren / Taxifahren ist ziemlich teuer.

Wenn die *-ing*-Form eines Verbs im Satz die Funktion eines **Nomens** hat, wird sie **Gerundium** *(gerund)* genannt. Die *-ing*-Form wird, wie du weißt, durch Anhängen von *-ing* an den Infinitiv gebildet: ***fly*** → ***flying***. Wie ein Verb kann das Gerundium erweitert werden, z. B. durch ein Objekt *(a taxi)* oder eine Orts- oder Zeitangabe *(in New York)*.

b) The gerund as subject and object

I **enjoy** living in a big city. I can't **imagine** living in the country. Ich wohne gern in einer Großstadt. Ich kann mir nicht vorstellen, auf dem Land zu leben.

When I got to Times Square, it **started** raining. / to rain.

I **like/love** riding / to ride my bike in the rain.

Das Gerundium (und seine Erweiterung) kann wie ein Nomen **Subjekt** oder **Objekt** eines Satzes sein:

<u>**Subjekt**</u>	
Flying	*is exciting.*
Cycling in a big city	*isn't very healthy.*
	<u>**Objekt**</u>
My sister likes	***skating.***
I like	***riding my bike in Central Park.***

◂ **1** Nach einigen Verben – z. B. ***enjoy, finish, imagine, miss, practise*** – muss ein weiteres Verb als Gerundium stehen: *I* ***enjoy*** *living ..., I can't* ***imagine*** *living ...*

◂ **2** Nach ***begin/start, continue, hate, like, love, prefer*** kann – bei gleicher Bedeutung – ein Gerundium oder ein *to*-Infinitiv stehen.

c) The gerund after prepositions

After so much walking, we were tired.
Nachdem wir so viel herumgelaufen waren, ...
Never cross a street without looking.
Überquere nie eine Straße, ohne zu schauen.
Ryan is **scared** of going in lifts.
Ryan hat Angst davor, mit dem Lift zu fahren.

Nach einer Präposition *(after, without, for, of, ...)* muss ein Verb als Gerundium stehen.
Beachte die unterschiedlichen Entsprechungen im Deutschen:

<u>englisch</u>		<u>deutsch</u>
– ***after walking***	→	**Präposition + Nomen** („nach ...") *oder* **Nebensatz** („nachdem ...")
– ***without looking***	→	„ohne zu" + **Infinitiv**
– *scared* ***of going***	→	„zu" + **Infinitiv**

Unit 2

GF 2 Conditional sentences

▸ *GF pp. 175–176*

a) REVISION Conditional sentences (type 1)

If Gracie is quiet, Mrs Tripp won't give her extra work. Wenn Gracie still ist, gibt Mrs Tripp ihr keine zusätzlichen Aufgaben.

Bedingungssätze vom Typ 1 (**„Was <u>ist</u>, wenn ..."-Sätze**) beziehen sich auf die **Gegenwart** oder die **Zukunft**.
Sie sagen aus, was unter bestimmten Bedingungen **geschieht** oder **nicht geschieht**.

b) REVISION Conditional sentences (type 2)

If Gracie was quiet, Mrs Tripp wouldn't give her extra work. Wenn Gracie still wäre, würde Mrs Tripp ihr keine zusätzlichen Aufgaben geben.

Bedingungssätze vom Typ 2 (**„Was <u>wäre</u>, wenn ..."-Sätze**) beziehen sich auch auf die **Gegenwart** oder die **Zukunft**.
Sie drücken aus, was unter bestimmten Bedingungen **geschehen** oder **nicht geschehen <u>würde</u>**.

c) Conditional sentences (type 3)

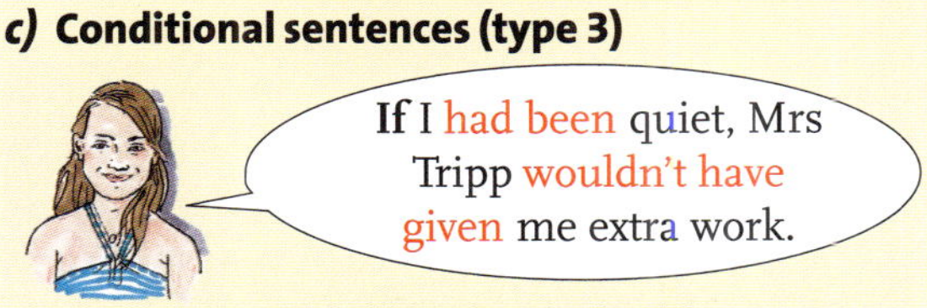

Wenn ich still gewesen wäre, hätte Mrs Tripp mir keine zusätzlichen Aufgaben gegeben.
If Mike hadn't told that stupid story, ...
... Gracie wouldn't have interrupted him.

Bedingungssätze vom Typ 3 sind **„Was <u>wäre gewesen</u>, wenn ..."-Sätze**. Sie beziehen sich auf die **Vergangenheit**.

Sie drücken aus, was **geschehen** oder **nicht geschehen <u>wäre</u>**, wenn eine Bedingung eingetreten wäre.

◂ Im ***if*-Satz** steht das ***past perfect*** *(hadn't told)*.
◂ Im **Hauptsatz** steht ***would(n't) + have*** **+ Partizip Perfekt** *(wouldn't have interrupted)*.

GF 3 Indirect speech ▸ *GF pp. 177–178*

a) REVISION Direct and indirect speech

Direct speech — Gracie's dad says, 'Plimoth Plantation is a living-history museum.'

Indirect speech (reporting verb: simple present) — Gracie's dad says (that) Plimoth Plantation is a living-history museum.

Indirect speech (reporting verb: simple past) — Gracie's dad said (that) Plimoth Plantation was a living-history museum.

In der **direkten Rede** wird **wörtlich** wiedergegeben, was jemand sagt, schreibt oder denkt.
In der **indirekten Rede** (*indirect* oder *reported speech*) wird berichtet, was jemand sagt, schreibt oder denkt.
Häufig vorkommende einleitende Verben sind *say, tell sb., answer, explain, believe, think.*
Wenn das **einleitende Verb im *simple past*** steht (*said, told sb., answered* usw.), dann werden die Zeitformen der direkten Rede meist verändert: Sie werden um eine Zeitstufe in die Vergangenheit „zurückverschoben" *(backshift of tenses).*

Reporting verb in the simple past ▸ backshift of tenses

present	▸	past	*will*-future	▸	*would* + infinitive
past	▸	past perfect	*going to*-future	▸	*was/were going to* + infinitive
present perfect	▸	past perfect	*can, may*	▸	*could, might*

b) Questions in indirect speech

Direct question (yes/no question) — Do tourists come to the plantation in winter too?
Indirect question — Gracie asked **if/whether tourists** came to the plantation in winter too.
Direct question (with question word) — **When** did the museum open?
Indirect question — She wanted to know **when** the museum had opened.

Auch bei Fragen in der indirekten Rede erfolgt der *backshift of tenses*, wenn das einleitende Verb im *simple past* steht.

Handelt es sich bei der direkten Frage um eine **Frage ohne Fragewort** *(yes/no question)*, dann wird die indirekte Frage mit ***if*** oder ***whether*** („ob") eingeleitet.

Wenn die direkte **Frage mit einem Fragewort** beginnt (*why, how, what, when, where* usw.), dann wird das Fragewort in der indirekten Frage beibehalten.

c) Commands and requests in indirect speech

Guide: 'Go back to the visitor center. And don't miss the movie.'
The guide told Gracie to go back to the visitor center. And she told her not to miss the movie.
Die Fremdenführerin sagte Gracie, sie solle zum Besucherzentrum zurückgehen ...

Aufforderungssätze werden in der indirekten Rede meist mit ***tell sb. to do sth.*** (bzw. ***tell sb. not to do sth.***) wiedergegeben.

Gracie: 'Can you give me a booklet about the exhibition, please?'
Gracie asked someone at the visitor center to give her a booklet about the exhibition.
Gracie bat jemanden ... zu geben.

Eine **Bitte** wird meist mit ***ask sb. to do sth.*** (bzw. ***ask sb. not to do sth.***) wiedergegeben.

Unit 3

GF 4 The passive ▸ *GF pp. 179–180*

b) Form

The passive

Simple present	Spanish is spoken by a lot of people in California. ... wird von vielen Menschen ... gesprochen
Simple past	In 1989, parts of San Francisco were destroyed by an earthquake. ... wurden zerstört
Present perfect	Relations between Anglos and Latinos have been improved by new laws. ... wurden verbessert/sind verbessert worden

Das Passiv bildest du mit einer **Form von *be*** und der 3. Form des Verbs (Partizip Perfekt, *past participle*).

***c)* The passive:**
***will*-future and modal auxiliaries**

These strawberries will be planted tomorrow.
... werden morgen gepflanzt werden.
Strawberries can be grown all the year round.
... können das ganze Jahr über angebaut werden.

Passivsätze mit Hilfsverben *(will, can, could, ...)* bildest du mit *be* + Partizip Perfekt:

will	***be***	***planted***
can	***be***	***grown***

***d)* The passive of verbs with two objects**

		Indirect object	Direct object
Active:	The teacher gave	Luis	an assignment.

Die Lehrerin gab Luis eine Hausarbeit auf.

Passive:

Dativobjekt		**Subjekt**	
Luis/Ihm	wurde	**eine Hausarbeit**	aufgegeben.

Subject
1 Luis/He was given **an assignment**.

Subject
2 **An assignment** was given to Luis.

Manche Verben haben zwei Objekte nach sich:
– ein **indirektes Objekt** (meist eine Person, daher auch: **Personenobjekt**) und ein
– **direktes Objekt** (meist eine Sache, daher auch: **Sachobjekt**).

Im Deutschen kann nur das **direkte Objekt** (das Sachobjekt) zum **Subjekt des Passivsatzes** werden.
Im Englischen kann
1 das **Personenobjekt** (hier: *Luis/He*) zum **Subjekt des Passivsatzes** werden. (Diese Art des Passivs nennt man *personal passive*, deutsch „persönliches Passiv".)
2 das **Sachobjekt** (hier: *an assignment*) zum **Subjekt des Passivsatzes** werden. (Beachte, dass das Personenobjekt in diesen Fällen mit *to* angehängt wird.)

GF 5 Participles

▸ *GF p. 181*

***a)* REVISION Participle forms**

Present participle *(-ing)*:

play	→ **playing**	try	→ **trying**
phone	→ **phoning**	plan	→ **planning**

Past participle, regular verbs *(-ed)*:

play	→ **played**	try	→ **tried**
phone	→ **phoned**	plan	→ **planned**

Past participle, irregular verbs:

go	→ **gone**	grow	→ **grown**

◂ Das **Partizip Präsens** *(present participle)* bildest du durch Anhängen von ***-ing*** an den Infinitiv.
Beachte die Besonderheiten bei der Schreibung.

◂ Das **Partizip Perfekt** *(past participle)* eines regelmäßigen Verbs wird durch Anhängen von ***-ed*** an den Infinitiv gebildet. Beachte auch hier die Besonderheiten bei der Schreibung.
Unregelmäßige Verben haben eigene 3. Formen, die du einzeln lernen musst.

***b)* Participle clauses instead of relative clauses**

1 Mrs Morales sat in the **bus** taking **her back to San Clemente.**
Mrs Morales saß im Bus, der sie ... zurückbrachte.
2 She spoke to the **children** playing **on the floor.**
... mit den Kindern, die auf dem Boden spielten
3 Have you ever eaten **strawberries** grown **in California**? ..., die in Kalifornien angebaut wurden?

Partizipialsätze können Relativsätze ersetzen.
◂ Das ***present participle*** (Sätze **1** und **2**) entspricht einem Relativpronomen + Verb im **Aktiv**:
1 ... *taking her back* = ... ***that was taking*** *her back*
2 ... *playing on the floor* = ... ***who were playing*** ...

◂ Das ***past participle*** (Satz **3**) entspricht einem Relativpronomen + Verb im **Passiv**:
3 ... *grown in California* = ... ***that were grown*** ...

GF 6 The *to*-infinitive

▸ *GF pp. 182–183*

***a)* Verb + object + *to*-infinitive**

The Clean Ocean Program flyer **asks** people not to leave garbage on the beaches. ... bittet die Leute, keinen Müll an den Stränden liegen zu lassen.
Luis's coach **would like** the class to help with the Clean Ocean Program.
... möchte, dass die Klasse ... mithilft.
He **told** them to find out about the program.
... dass sie sich über das Programm informieren sollten.
The flyer says, 'We **want** you to help us.'
... „Wir wollen, dass du uns hilfst."

Nach bestimmten Verben kann ein **Objekt + *to*-Infinitiv** stehen, z.B. *ask/help/invite/teach sb. (not) to do sth.*
Im Deutschen steht meist ein Infinitiv mit „zu":
jn. bitten/jm. helfen/..., etwas (nicht) zu tun.
◂ Auch nach den Verben *cause, tell, want, would like* kann ein **Objekt + *to*-Infinitiv** stehen.
! Nach den entsprechenden deutschen Verben steht ein Nebensatz mit „dass", aber auf die englischen Verben darf kein *that*-Satz folgen:
*Wir **wollen**, dass du uns hilfst. We **want** you to help us.*
Nicht: *We want ~~that you help~~ us.*

***b)* Question word + *to*-infinitive**

Luis When we saw all the garbage, we wanted to help. But we didn't **know** what to do.
... Aber wir wussten nicht, was wir tun sollten.

Der *to*-Infinitiv steht oft nach einem **Fragewort** (*what, who, how, when, where* usw.). Er entspricht meist einem Nebensatz mit modalem Hilfsverb *(can, could, should, ...)*.

Unit 4

GF 7 Countable and uncountable nouns

▸ *GF pp. 183–184*

***b)* Uncountable nouns**

bread *Brot*	**jewellery** *Schmuck*
butter *Butter*	**milk** *Milch*
experience *Erfahrung(en)*	**money** *Geld*
furniture *Möbel*	**mustard** *Senf*
homework *Hausaufgabe(n)*	**news** *Nachricht(en)*
information *Information(en)*	**traffic** *Verkehr*

That's too much **homework**. I can't do it.
Das sind zu viele **Hausaufgaben**. Ich kann sie nicht ...
Would you like a glass of **milk**.
Möchtest du **ein Glas Milch**?

Nicht zählbare Nomen bezeichnen etwas, das man nicht zählen kann. Dazu gehören viele Bezeichnungen für Lebensmittel und viele abstrakte Begriffe.

! Auch die Nomen ***experience, furniture, homework, information*** und ***news*** sind nicht zählbar – anders als ihre deutschen Entsprechungen.
Die zugehörigen **Begleiter, Verben und Pronomen** stehen immer **im Singular**.
Wenn du **bestimmte Mengen** oder eine **bestimmte Anzahl** nennen willst, musst du passende Wendungen wie ***a glass of ..., a kilo of ..., a piece of ...*** verwenden.

***c)* Quantifiers:**
some, a lot of, many, much, a few, a little

Countable nouns	Uncountable nouns
some **students**	some **bread/information**
einige/ein paar ...	etwas Brot/einige Informationen
a lot of **students**	a lot of **bread/information**
viele ...	viel Brot/viele Informationen
how many **students?**	**how** much **bread/information?**
wie viele ...?	wie viel Brot? / wie viele Informationen?
a few **students**	a little **bread**
wenige/ein paar ...	wenig/ein bisschen Brot

Die Mengenangaben *some* und *a lot of* (oder *lots of*) verwendest du sowohl mit dem **Plural von zählbaren Nomen** als auch mit **nicht zählbaren Nomen**.

! – *many* („**viele**") steht nur mit dem **Plural** von zählbaren Nomen.
much („**viel**") steht nur mit **nicht zählbaren Nomen**.
– *a few* („**wenige/ein paar**") steht nur mit dem **Plural** von zählbaren Nomen.
a little („**wenig/ein bisschen**") steht nur mit **nicht zählbaren Nomen**.

GF 8 The definite article *the*

▸ *GF p. 185*

1 For Timo and his family, life is exciting at the moment. ... ist das Leben im Moment aufregend.
2 Clean air is important to health.
Saubere Luft ist wichtig für die Gesundheit.
3 American students do lots of extracurricular activities.
1a At the FFA meeting Timo learned a lot about the life **of Missouri farmers**.
... über das Leben der Farmer in Missouri.

Wenn ein Nomen **ganz allgemein** gebraucht wird, steht es **ohne den bestimmten Artikel** (auch, wenn ein Adjektiv davor steht). Das gilt insbesondere für

1 **abstrakte Begriffe** wie *life, history, health, quality*
2 **Stoffbezeichnungen** wie *air, oil, gold, wine*
3 **Nomen im Plural** (hier: *students*).

Solche Nomen stehen jedoch **mit bestimmtem Artikel**, wenn sie **näher bestimmt** sind, z.B. durch eine *of*-Fügung.

Unit 5

GF 10 Relative clauses

▸ *GF pp. 186–187*

***a)* REVISION Defining relative clauses**

1 Madison knew the **people** who/that worked at the King Center.
2 She was interested in the **letters** which/that were on display in the Center.

Bestimmende Relativsätze werden mit den Relativpronomen
– *who* oder *that* für Personen **(1)** und
– *which* oder *that* für Dinge **(2)** eingeleitet.
Ein bestimmender Relativsatz gibt Informationen über ein Nomen, die **zum Verständnis des Satzes notwendig** sind.

***b)* ... *which* to refer to a whole clause**

Mom had to go to the airport to report on a big fire, which sounded pretty exciting to me.
..., was sich ziemlich aufregend anhörte.

Relativsätze mit *which* können sich auch auf einen ganzen Satz beziehen. Mit solchen Relativsätzen wird die Aussage im vorausgehenden Hauptsatz kommentiert.